4₴

SHAW ON RELIGION

SHAW
ON RELIGION

*Edited with Introduction
and Notes by
Warren Sylvester Smith*

DODD, MEAD & COMPANY
NEW YORK

Contents

[Note: In all of the selections from Shaw's works, his own individual orthography, punctuation, capitalization, etc., have been generally retained.]

Introduction

This book is offered less as a historical curiosity that ought rightly to have appeared thirty-five years ago than as a fresh entry into the current religious dialogue. It is, however, something of both.

The Standard Edition of Bernard Shaw's Collected Works first appeared in 1930. Among the non-dramatic volumes (such as *Pen Portraits and Reviews*), Shaw intended one devoted to his uncollected writings on religious subjects. It was to bear the title *Religion and Religions*. The table of contents still exists in the British Museum, along with proof-read and amended copies of the articles Shaw had selected for inclusion. The portfolio contains three items marked 'hitherto unpublished', as well as some fugitive pieces that might easily escape a careful collector. These are retained here (even at the expense of some repetition), and with them are included whatever from the plays, prefaces, and letters seemed necessary to the Essential Religious Shaw. For if the book is to serve its wider purpose of contributing to the present debate-in-progress, the reader may need some help in culling from the thirty or forty volumes, none of which are without pertinent material. Shaw was a deeply religious writer and his own peculiar mysticism infuses everything he wrote.

Very possibly, therefore, I have left out the favourite passage of many a convinced Shavian. But, as I say, the book is not primarily for him. It is for the rebellious seeker who has considered – at least second-hand, and perhaps without knowing it – the views of Karl Barth, Paul Tillich, Rudolph Bultmann and Dietrich Bonhoeffer.

These theologians have largely reached the general public through intermediaries. The most recent popular break-through in the ancient exchange began three years ago with the Bishop of Woolwich's *Honest to God*, and has been kept simmering since then by the series of *Objections (to Christian Belief, to Humanism, to Roman Catholicism)* and dozens of other books and articles, erupting in America, even as I write, into inch-and-a-half red letters on the cover of *Time*: IS GOD DEAD?

Now whether or not Bernard Shaw qualifies as a theologian, he certainly qualifies as a popular writer and needs no intermediary. What he has to say he says to anyone who can read. The pertinent introductory question, therefore, is whether G. B. Shaw, who was born in the 1850s, formed his religious ideas in the 1860s and 70s, became articulate in the 80s, and after unprecedented loquacity through seven decades died, finally, in 1950, has anything requisite to contribute to a religious discussion of the 1960s.

It is worth pausing, first, to ask what are the hallmarks of the popular side of the discussion as it now stands.

As to the basic theological question, the 'God Up There' or 'Out There' as Bishop Robinson has labelled Him, has completely vanished. Thinking people have quietly, if reluctantly, answered the big red letters, 'Yes, I'm afraid so,' unless they have been successful in redefining the term 'God' as something like 'the ultimate reality'.[1] Indeed, respectable churchmen now dare to ask the question, 'Is

[1] John A. R. Robinson, *Honest to God* (S.C.M.P., 1963), p. 29.

there really a connection between religion and self-realiza-
tion?' And they have taken to calling such a question
existential, mainly, it seems, because they have, like
Ecclesiastes, despaired of ever finding an answer, and because it is currently a safe word to use. Those who hang
fast to Christian doctrine insist that it must, in any case, be
'demythologized' if it is to be useful. The bare recital of the
atonement myth, says J. S. Bezzant, 'has the aspect of a
malicious travesty'.[2] The old myths are palatable only in so
far as they illustrate the concept that 'there is no doctrine
of Christianity which is not dimly perceived in the racial
consciousness'.[3]

Religious morality, which used to dictate our ethics, must
now make its peace with modern psychology. The old
legalism has necessarily disappeared with the God Out
There, who was the ultimate enforcer of it. He failed to
enforce it when 'the God of Abraham did not save his
people at Belsen, and for the victims of the Allies at Dresden
Christ and his saints slept'.[4] Though Sin is an unpopular
concept, Guilt is much in vogue, and hangs over the controversy, searching for liberation. Without its pressure to
keep it alive the entire discourse would deflate. As a standard
for ethical or moral behaviour 'love' has become too
ambiguous to be useful. Still, it is evident that in the new
morality ethics must be individual and relative. 'Caring
enough,' says Bishop Robinson, 'is the criterion for every
form of behaviour.... *Nothing else* makes it right or
wrong.'[5]

[2] in *Objections to Christian Belief* (Constable, 1963), p. 84.
[3] G. F. Pollard in *Objections to Roman Catholicism* (Constable, 1964), p. 162.
[4] Magdalen Goffin in *Objections to Roman Catholicism*, pp.
35–6.
[5] *Honest to God*, p. 119. Emphasis his.

9

In the midst of this the Church as an organization or an authority would seem to be in disarray, though, paradoxically, it may be adding members. Even as a historical entity which began in A.D. 170, it has been found by modern historians to be so full of schisms, backtracking, and inconsistencies as to be of little use in honest guidance. Certainly, as Rosemary Haughton expresses it, the Rock is shuddering and the safe refuge is about to erupt.[6] Partly in need of security, partly in response to its own collective sense of guilt, the Church has lately shown signs of pulling itself together, even while many an individual member seeks out a little room of his own as refuge from the spiritual chaos.

These are, it seems to me, the essential charges against conventional theology, conventional morality, the conventional Church. Can the old sage of Ayot possibly have anything to say about them out of the dim pre-atomic past?

A good Shavian would probably hasten at this point to declare that since Shaw was roughly fifty years ahead of his time, the world is only now catching up with his early-century pronouncements. And in most respects this would be perfectly true. But a past prophet, no matter how percipient, cannot safely be read as a contemporary. And Shaw's value to the discussion is not in terms of the answers he gives (which are no longer surprisingly different from those of many liberal theologians), but in his *manner* of looking at the problems. The special quality of the light he throws is unique and likely to remain so.

A number of times Shaw tells the story of his encounter with the phrenologist. You will find one version among the following selections in 'The Infancy of God'. The punchline in all versions is that where the phrenologist should have found the bump of veneration on Shaw's head he found instead a hole. I don't know whether the actual

[6] *Objections to Roman Catholicism*, p. 114.

incident ever took place, but the moral of the yarn is true. Unlike the churchman who is either defending his creed or revolting from it, unlike the militantly atheistic Bible-smasher of the 1870s and 80s, Shaw is detached, having no veneration to assault or protect.

As a child he could enjoy, apparently without any sense of guilt, his uncle's ribald story of how Jesus was last seen running down the other side of the hill of Calvary with his coat-tails flying. The piquancy of Shaw's later style grew from the sense that he was a 'sojourner on this planet, not a native of it'. He was the Complete Outsider. And this same alienation which was also the effortless source of his humour gives many of his comments clarity and candour that ought still to be welcome. Only the keenest of his con-temporaries (like G. K. Chesterton) took the religious Shaw seriously. ('. . . in a sweeter and more solid civilization he would have been a great saint.') Most religionists who found themselves in debate with him never realized that he was really on their side; that he fought atheism in his own manner; that he was a natural mystic who happened also to have a sense of humour.

On the other hand such radical contemporaries of his youth as were represented by the National Secular Society abandoned all notions of divinity when they abandoned the 'God Up There'. They could as readily comprehend the multiplication of the loaves and fishes as Shaw's Divine Immanence, which he was content to call, near the end of his life, Divine Providence. Many, like the Positivist follow-ers of Comte, turned to Science or Humanity as the new God. Shaw was as sceptical of scientists as he was of priests and had little of the romantic faith in the future of humanity that so exalted Winwood Reade or Edward Bellamy. But though his belief in progress waned, so that after the First World War he was tempted to despair, he could not turn to cynicism or that complete sense of impotence which in the hands of Samuel Beckett seemed to give some kind of satisfaction – or at least expression – to the decade of the 1950s. The last two sentences in this collection, written in the last year of Shaw's life, are evidence of a nature that cannot give up the fight, and like Valiant-for-truth must pass on his courage and skill to him that can get them.

The Bergsonian Life Force has not been, it is true, a popular replacement for the Judeo-Christian divinity, but in review this may be less because it lacks the transcendent attributes of the old God – most of which have tacitly disappeared from modern thought in any case – than because it seems, on the surface at least, too over-simplified a statement of evolutionary theory. As for demythologizing, who else has 'searched the racial consciousness' to give a sample of what the new myths are to be like by way of a 'meta-biological pentateuch'?

Consider now what is still called 'the new morality'. If Shaw did not invent it, he was one of its first Victorian advocates. Yet our present liberated generation may find it bracing to come into contact with his ascetic Puritanism. For Shaw's morality was individual, but not lax. He supported the right of Ibsen's Nora to walk out on her husband and children, but only in the cause of making her a better woman, a more complete person. She chose a greater, not a lesser, responsibility. Personal behaviour, for Shaw, is always tied to the social ethic. The freest of modern sex practices would not of themselves have shocked him. But the cruelty, the inefficiency, the lack of direction of our era would have continued both to shock and sadden him in any of their manifestations.

For himself Shaw did not need a Church any more than Bertrand Russell or Julian Huxley does – though he sometimes appreciated the empty buildings. He nevertheless

understood the common need to gather and worship. Consequently his life-long wrangling with vicars and bishops and
deans and nonconformist parsons was always in the direction of building a Church in which all intelligent seekers
could worship together. He was all the more severe in his
scoldings because his aim was not destruction but reformation – though reformation in such extent that prior destruction must often have seemed as easy an alternative. His
response to Margaret Ponsonby's query on closing the
churches (p. 130) and the opening paragraph of *On Ritual,
Religion* . . . (p. 148) make the point clearly.

Indeed in all these matters Shaw's own words are more
than adequate. I have merely wanted to show that the
subject-matter is in fact that of the current religious debate.
Whether it speaks, as the Quakers say, to the reader's condition, the reader himself will have to determine.

The selections that follow are arranged chronologically.
They begin when Shaw was forty years old. Emotionally
detached and uncommitted as we have maintained he was
from an early age, he always looked in on the religious
phenomenon with uncommon interest, perhaps by virtue of
his having been a 'bloody Protestant' in the midst of
Catholic Dublin ('a *sanguinary* Protestant' is the way
Puritan Shaw put it in public). He has on several occasions
reminisced on his religious upbringing, most entertainingly
in his autobiographical Preface to *Immaturity*, from which
I shall quote here only his recollection of childhood prayer
to which he alludes briefly in his essay *On Ritual,
Religion.* . . . :

In my childhood I exercised my literary genius by com-
posing my own prayers. I cannot recall the words of the

final form I adopted; but I remember that it was in three movements, like a sonata, and in the best Church of Ireland style. It ended with the Lord's Prayer; and I repeated it every night in bed. I had been warned by my nurse that warm prayers were no use, and that only by kneeling by my bedside in the cold could I hope for a hearing; but I criticized this admonition unfavourably on various grounds, the real one being my preference for warmth and comfort. I did not disparage my nurse's authority in these matters because she was a Roman Catholic; I even tolerated her practice of sprinkling me with holy water occasionally. But her asceticism did not fit the essentially artistic and luxurious character of my devotional exploits. Besides, the penalty did not apply to my prayer; for it was not a petition. I had too much sense to risk my faith by begging for things I knew very well I should not get; so I did not care whether my prayers were answered or not: they were a literary performance for the entertainment and propitiation of the Almighty; and though I should not have dreamt of daring to say that if He did not like them He might lump them (perhaps I was too confident of their quality to apprehend such a rebuff), I certainly behaved as if my comfort were an indispensable condition of the performance taking place at all.

Shaw's biographer, the late Archibald Henderson, once wrote me that if 'Sonny' Shaw had not been removed from Church when he was ten he would have become a faithful Church member instead of a recusant one. I cannot accept Pavlovian conditioning to such an extent. If Shaw had been kept in Church longer his separation might have been more explosive, but it would certainly have come. As it was, his baptism into the Church of Ireland was merely a mark of

snobbish class-consciousness which destined him to a boyhood of genteel poverty with all the pretensions that went
with it.

It is significant to note, as Anthony S. Abbott does in his
recent study of *Shaw and Christianity*,[7] that Shaw's literary
career began at the age of nineteen with the publication of
his letter to the Editor of Dublin's *Public Opinion* (signed
'S.'), commenting on the more secular aspects of the local
success of the travelling American revivalist team of Moody
and Sankey.

There has recently come to light another early manu-
script to tantalize biographers. With the mass of literary
remnants bequeathed to the British Museum at Shaw's
death, is a folder marked 'Juvenilia', containing a forty-
nine-page fragment of a 'Passion Play' in blank verse! It
was written and abandoned in the second year after Shaw
had come to London, 1878, when he was twenty-two. Its
title is *The Household of Joseph* and it begins promisingly
with a cast of characters headed: 'Jesus, illegitimate son of
Mary'. Mary is a shrew, Joseph a harmless drunkard, and
Jesus a renegade carpenter's apprentice who wastes his time
lying in the fields spinning yarns for the spiritual edification
of the townsfolk, until he is lured away from Nazareth to
the big city of Jerusalem by a sophisticated stranger named
Judas Iscariot, who brings him news, among other things,
of John the Baptist. I will not tempt the reader further
along this fascinating by-way except to say that the verse
seems to me more Shelleyan than Shakespearean, and that
the household bears more than passing resemblance to that
of George Carr Shaw and Lucy Shaw, with G. J. Vandeleur
Lee cast as Judas, leaving, quite naturally, young George
Bernard as Jesus, about to cross the Irish Sea and conquer
his own Jerusalem – or be crucified there. It is an adolescent

[7] New York, 1965.

image, but the images of adolescence can be, and often are, powerful and persistent.

The story of his passage through the stormy decades of journalistic pamphleteering and debate – much of it religious debate – is told elsewhere. His writings of the 80s and early 90s are not without reference to these matters, but it is not until 1896 that he again picks up the subject with both hands, this time as an adult. From this point on through half a century he speaks for himself.

Warren Sylvester Smith
Lemont, Pennsylvania

Jeremiah said long ago that the Word was as a burning fire shut up in his bones, and he was weary of forbearing and must speak. I have never felt so volcanic as Jeremiah, because I have never intensified my internal fires by forbearing; I have given my message free outlet at an even temperature: but I have only guided the pen of the Life Force as the husbandman guides its plough; and my only pride in the matter is to write legibly and tempt the world to read with the cunning that we call the writer's word.

A deleted passage from a discarded Preface to the Collected Works by Bernard Shaw.

(British Museum, 50664)

On Going to Church

In his 1896 essay, *On Going to Church*, Shaw maintained that the spiritual life of his contemporaries was kept alive chiefly by stimulants and drugs; however, church-going, if the churches were beautiful, and if they could be divorced from the intolerable services and creeds associated with them, might be a more natural and efficacious source of inspiration. His boyhood dream of going to heaven he later transferred to the character Tom Broadbent in the last act of *John Bull's Other Island*.

There is still one serious obstacle to the use of churches on the very day when most people are best able and most disposed to visit them. I mean, of course, the services. When I was a little boy, I was compelled to go to church on Sunday; and though I escaped from that intolerable bondage before I was ten, it prejudiced me so violently against church-going that twenty years elapsed before, in foreign lands and in pursuit of works of art, I became once more a churchgoer. To this day, my flesh creeps when I recall that genteel suburban Irish Protestant church, built by Roman Catholic workmen who would have considered themselves damned had they crossed its threshold afterwards. Every separate stone, every pane of glass, every fillet of ornamental ironwork –

half-dog-collar, half-coronet – in that building must have
sowed a separate evil passion in my young heart. Yes; all
the vulgarity, savagery, and bad blood which has marred
my literary work, was certainly laid upon me in that house
of Satan! The mere nullity of the building could make no
positive impression on me; but what could, and did, were
the unnaturally motionless figures of the congregation in
their Sunday clothes and bonnets, and their set faces, pale
with the malignant rigidity produced by the suppression of
all expression. And yet these people were always moving
and watching one another by stealth, as convicts communi-
cate with one another. So was I. I had been told to keep my
restless little limbs still all through those interminable hours;
not to talk; and, above all, to be happy and holy there and
glad that I was not a wicked little boy playing in the fields
instead of worshipping God. I hypocritically acquiesced; but
the state of my conscience may be imagined, especially as I
implicitly believed that all the rest of the congregation were
perfectly sincere and good. I remember at that time dreaming one night that I was dead and had gone to heaven. The
picture of heaven which the efforts of the then Established
Church of Ireland had conveyed to my childish imagination
was a waiting room with walls of pale sky-coloured tabbinet,
and a pew-like bench running all round, except at one corner, where there was a door. I was, somehow, aware that
God was in the next room, accessible through that door. I
was seated on the bench with my ankles tightly interlaced
to prevent my legs dangling, behaving myself with all my
might before the grown-up people, who all belonged to the
Sunday congregation, and were either sitting on the bench
as if at church or else moving solemnly in and out as if there
were a dead person in the house. A grimly-handsome lady
who usually sat in a corner seat near me in church, and
whom I believed to be thoroughly conversant with the

arrangements of the Almighty, was to introduce me
presently into the next room – a moment which I was supposed to await with joy and enthusiasm. Really, of course,
my heart sank like lead within me at the thought; for I felt
that my feeble affectation of piety could not impose on
Omniscience, and that one glance of that all-searching eye
would discover that I had been allowed to come to heaven
by mistake. Unfortunately for the interest of this narrative,
I awoke, or wandered off into another dream, before the
critical moment arrived. But it goes far enough to show that
I was by no means an insusceptible subject: indeed, I am
sure, from other early experiences of mine, that if I had
been turned loose in a real church, and allowed to wander
and stare about, or hear noble music there instead of that
most accursed Te Deum of Jackson's and a senseless droning
of the Old Hundredth, I should never have seized the
opportunity of a great evangelical revival, which occurred
when I was still in my teens, to begin my literary career with
a letter to the Press (which was duly printed), announcing
with inflexible materialistic logic, and to the extreme horror
of my respectable connections, that I was an atheist. When,
later on, I was led to the study of the economic basis of the
respectability of that and similar congregations, I was in-
expressibly relieved to find that it represented a mere passing
phase of industrial confusion, and could never have sub-
stantiated its claims to my respect if, as a child, I had been
able to bring it to book. To this very day, whenever there is
the slightest danger of my being mistaken for a votary of
the blue tabbinet waiting-room or a supporter of that
morality in which wrong and right, base and noble, evil and
good, really mean nothing more than the kitchen and the
drawing-room, I hasten to claim honourable exemption, as
atheist and socialist, from any such complicity.

When I at last took to church-going again, a kindred

difficulty beset me, especially in Roman Catholic countries. In Italy, for instance, churches are used in such a way that priceless pictures become smeared with filthy tallow-soot, and have sometimes to be rescued by the temporal power and placed in national galleries. But worse than this are the innumerable daily services which disturb the truly religious visitor. If these were decently and intelligently conducted by genuine mystics to whom the Mass was no mere rite or miracle, but a real communion, the celebrants might reasonably claim a place in the church as their share of the common human right to its use. But the average Italian priest, personally uncleanly, and with chronic catarrh of the nose and throat, produced and maintained by sleeping and living in frowsy, ill-ventilated rooms, punctuating his gabbled Latin only by expectorative hawking, and making the decent guest sicken and shiver every time the horrible splash of spitten mucus echoes along the vaulting from the marble steps of the altar: this unseemly wretch should be seized and put out, bell, book, candle and all, until he learns to behave himself. The English tourist is often lectured for his inconsiderate behaviour in Italian churches, for walking about during service, talking loudly, thrusting himself rudely between a worshipper and an altar to examine a painting, even for stealing chips of stone and scrawling his name on statues. But as far as the mere disturbance of the services is concerned, and the often very evident disposition of the tourist – especially the experienced tourist – to regard the priest and his congregation as troublesome intruders, a week spent in Italy will convince any unprejudiced person that this is a perfectly reasonable attitude. I have seen inconsiderate British behaviour often enough both in church and out of it. The slow-witted Englishman who refuses to get out of the way of the Host, and looks at the bellringer going before it with 'Where the devil are you shoving to?' written

22

in every pucker of his free-born British brow, is a familiar
figure to me; but I have never seen any stranger behave so
insufferably as the officials of the church habitually do. It is
the sacristan who teaches you, when once you are committed
to tipping him, not to waste your good manners on the
kneeling worshippers who are snatching a moment from
their daily round of drudgery and starvation to be com-
forted by the Blessed Virgin or one of the saints: it is the
officiating priest who makes you understand that the congregation are past shocking by any indecency that you
would dream of committing, and that the black looks of the
congregation are directed at the foreigner and the heretic
only, and imply a denial of your right as a human being to
your share of the use of the church. That right should be
unflinchingly asserted on all proper occasions. I know no
contrary right by which the great Catholic churches made
for the world by the great church-builders should be mono-
polized by any sect as against any man who desires to use
them. My own faith is clear: I am a resolute Protestant;
I believe in the Holy Catholic Church; in the Holy Trinity
of Father, Son (or Mother, Daughter) and Spirit; in the
Communion of Saints, the Life to Come, the Immaculate
Conception, and the everyday reality of Godhead and the
Kingdom of Heaven. Also, I believe that salvation depends
on redemption from belief in miracles; and I regard St
Athanasius as an irreligious fool – that is, in the only serious
sense of the word, a damned fool. I pity the poor neurotic
who can say, 'Man that is born of a woman hath but a
short time to live, and is full of misery', as I pity a maudlin
drunkard; and I know that the real religion of today was
made possible only by the materialistic-physicists and atheist-
critics who performed for us the indispensable preliminary
operation of purging us thoroughly of the ignorant and
vicious superstitions which were thrust down our throats as

23

religion in our helpless childhood. How those who assume that our churches are the private property of their sect would think of this profession of faith of mine I need not describe. But am I, therefore, to be denied access to the place of spiritual recreation which is my inheritance as much as theirs? If, for example, I desire to follow a good old custom by pledging my love to my wife in the church of our parish, why should I be denied due record in the registers unless she submits to have a moment of deep feeling made ridiculous by the reading aloud of the *naïve* impertinences of St Peter, who, on the subject of Woman, was neither Catholic nor Christian, but a boorish Syrian fisherman. If I want to name a child in the church, the prescribed service may be more touched with the religious spirit – once or twice beautifully touched – but, on the whole, it is time to dismiss our prayer-book as quite rotten with the pessimism of the age which prescribed it. In spite of the stolen jewels with which it is studded, an age of strength and faith and noble activity can have nothing to do with it: Caliban might have constructed such a ritual out of his own terror of the supernatural, and such fragments of the words of the saints as he could dimly feel some sort of glory in.

My demand will now be understood without any cere-monious formulation of it. No nation, working at the strain we face, can live cleanly without public-houses in which to seek refreshment and recreation. To supply that vital want we have the drinking-shop with its narcotic, stimulant poisons, the conventicle with its brimstone-flavoured hot gospel, and the church. In the church alone can our need be truly met, nor even there save when we leave outside the door the materialisms that help us to think the unthinkable, completing the refuse-heap of 'isms' and creeds with our vain lust for truth and happiness, and going in without thought or belief or prayer or any other vanity, so that the soul, freed from all that crushing lumber, may open all its avenues of life to the holy air of the true Catholic Church.

[1896]

Preface to Man and Superman

Shaw's first major effort to tie the evolutionary theme to a mystical religious belief came in 1901–1903 in *Man and Superman*, especially in the third act dream sequence where Don Juan confronts the Devil. In the long 'Epistle Dedicatory' to Arthur Bingham Walkley which forms the Preface, Shaw establishes the presence of the mysterious Life Force. This force works unceasingly and perhaps unnoticed; but those who are most conscious of carrying out its purpose are the artists, who, like women, have been equipped by Nature to transmit its will to the future. Their effectiveness in doing so must form the first standard in any value-judgment of their works. This is the basis of Shaw's preference for Bunyan over Shakespeare.

Put your Shakespearean hero and coward, Henry V and Pistol or Parolles, beside Mr Valiant and Mr Fearing, and you have a sudden revelation of the abyss that lies between the fashionable author who could see nothing in the world but personal aims and the tragedy of their disappointment or the comedy of their incongruity, and the field preacher who achieved virtue and courage by identifying himself with the purpose of the world as he understood it. The contrast is enormous: Bunyan's coward stirs your blood more than Shakespear's hero, who actually leaves you cold and secretly hostile. You suddenly see that Shakespear, with all his flashes and divinations, never understood virtue and courage, never conceived how any man who was not a fool could, like Bunyan's hero, look back from the brink of the river of death over the strife and labour of his pilgrimage, and say 'yet do I not repent me'; or, with the panache of a millionaire, bequeath 'my sword to him that shall succeed me in my pilgrimage, and my courage and skill to him that can get it.' This is the true joy in life, the being used for a purpose recognized by yourself as a mighty one; the being thoroughly worn out before you are thrown on the scrap heap; the being a force of Nature instead of a feverish selfish little clod of ailments and grievances complaining that the world will not devote itself to making you happy. And also the only real tragedy in life is the being used by personally minded men for purposes which you recognize to be base. All the rest is at worst mere misfortune or mortality: this alone is misery, slavery, hell on earth; and the revolt against it is the only force that offers a man's work to the poor artist, whom our personally minded rich people would so willingly employ as pandar, buffoon, beauty monger, sentimentalizer and the like.

It may seem a long step from Bunyan to Nietzsche; but the difference between their conclusions is merely formal. Bunyan's perception that righteousness is filthy rags, his scorn for Mr Legality in the village of Morality, his defiance of the Church as the supplanter of religion, his insistence on courage as the virtue of virtues, his estimate of the career of the conventionally respectable and sensible Worldly Wiseman as no better at bottom than the life and death of Mr Badman: all this, expressed by Bunyan in the terms of a tinker's theology, is what Nietzsche has expressed in terms of post-Darwin, post-Schopenhauer philosophy; Wagner in terms of polytheistic mythology; and Ibsen in terms of mid-

XIX-century Parisian dramaturgy. Nothing is new in these matters except their novelties: for instance, it is a novelty to call Justification by Faith 'Wille', and Justification by Works 'Vorstellung'. The sole use of the novelty is that you and I buy and read Schopenhauer's treatise on Will and Representation when we should not dream of buying a set of sermons on Faith versus Works. At bottom the controversy is the same, and the dramatic results are the same. Bunyan makes no attempt to present his pilgrims as more sensible or better conducted than Mr Worldly Wiseman. Mr W.W.'s worst enemies, Mr Embezzler, Mr Never-go-to-Church-on-Sunday, Mr Bad Form, Mr Murderer, Mr Burglar, Mr Co-respondent, Mr Blackmailer, Mr Cad, Mr Drunkard, Mr Labour Agitator and so forth, can read The Pilgrim's Progress without finding a word said against them; whereas the respectable people who snub them and put them in prison, such as Mr W.W. himself and his young friend Civility; Formalist and Hypocrisy; Wildhead, Inconsiderate, and Pragmatick (who were clearly young university men of good family and high feeding); that brisk lad Ignorance, Talkative, By-ends of Fairspeech and his mother-in-law Lady Feigning, and other reputable gentlemen and citizens, catch it very severely. Even Little Faith, though he gets to heaven at last, is given to understand that it served him right to be mobbed by the brothers Faint Heart, Mistrust, and Guilt, all three recognized members of respectable society and veritable pillars of the law. The whole allegory is a consistent attack on morality and respectability, without a word that one can remember against vice and crime. Exactly what is complained of in Nietzsche and Ibsen, is it not? And also exactly what would be complained of in all the literature which is great enough and old enough to have attained canonical rank, officially or unofficially, were it not that books are admitted to the canon by a compact which

28

confesses their greatness in consideration of abrogating their meaning; so that the reverend rector can agree with the prophet Micah as to his inspired style without being committed to any complicity in Micah's furiously Radical opinions. Why, even I, as I force myself, pen in hand, into recognition and civility, find all the force of my onslaught destroyed by a simple policy of non-resistance. In vain do I redouble the violence of the language in which I proclaim my heterodoxies. I rail at the theistic credulity of Voltaire, the amoristic superstition of Shelley, the revival of tribal soothsaying and idolatrous rites which Huxley called Science and mistook for an advance on the Pentateuch, no less than at the welter of ecclesiastical and professional humbug which saves the face of the stupid system of violence and robbery which we call Law and Industry. Even atheists reproach me with infidelity and anarchists with nihilism because I cannot endure their moral tirades. And yet, instead of exclaiming 'Send this inconceivable Satanist to the stake', the respectable newspapers pith me by announcing 'another book by this brilliant and thoughtful writer'. And the ordinary citizen, knowing that an author who is well spoken of by a respectable newspaper must be all right, reads me, as he reads Micah, with undisturbed edification from his own point of view. It is narrated that in the eighteen-seventies an old lady, a very devout Methodist, moved from Colchester to a house in the neighbourhood of the City Road, in London, where, mistaking the Hall of Science for a chapel, she sat at the feet of Charles Bradlaugh for many years, entranced by his eloquence, without questioning his orthodoxy or moulting a feather of her faith. I fear I shall be defrauded of my just martyrdom in the same way.

[1903]

Man and Superman

Though, in the dream sequence of *Man and Superman*, the Life Force speaks through Don Juan, Shaw gives him a creditable antagonist in the Devil. The Devil is here, in essence, the Darwinian determinist, the acceptor of a mechanistic universe.

THE DEVIL. Don Juan: shall I be frank with you?

DON JUAN. Were you not so before?

THE DEVIL. As far as I went, yes. But I will now go further, and confess to you that men get tired of everything, of heaven no less than of hell; and that all history is nothing but a record of the oscillations of the world between these two extremes. An epoch is but a swing of the pendulum; and each generation thinks the world is progressing because it is always moving. But when you are as old as I am; when you have a thousand times wearied of heaven, like myself and the Commander, and a thousand times wearied of hell, as you are wearied now, you will no longer imagine that every swing from heaven to hell is an emancipation, every swing from hell to heaven an evolution. Where you now see reform, progress, fulfilment of upward tendency, continual ascent by Man on the stepping-stones of his dead selves to higher things, you will see nothing but an infinite comedy of illusion. You will discover the profound truth of the saying of my friend Koheleth, that there is nothing new under the sun. Vanitas vanitatum –

DON JUAN [*out of all patience*] By Heaven, this is worse than your cant about love and beauty. Clever dolt that you are, is a man no better than a worm, or a dog than a wolf, because he gets tired of everything? Shall he give up eating because he destroys his appetite in the act of gratifying it? Is a field idle when it is fallow? Can the Commander expand his hellish energy here without accumulating heavenly energy for his next term of blessedness? Granted that the great Life Force has hit on the device of the clockmaker's pendulum, and uses the earth for its bob; that the history of each oscillation, which seems so novel to us the actors, is but the history of the last oscillation repeated; nay more, that in the unthinkable infinitude of time the sun throws off the earth and catches it again a thousand times as a circus rider throws up a ball, and that our agelong epochs are but the moments between the toss and the catch, has the colossal mechanism no purpose?

THE DEVIL. None, my friend. You think, because you have a purpose, Nature must have one. You might as well expect it to have fingers and toes because you have them.

DON JUAN. But I should not have them if they served no purpose. And I, my friend, am as much a part of Nature as my own finger is a part of me. If my finger is the organ by which I grasp the sword and the mandoline, my brain is the organ by which Nature strives to understand itself. My dog's brain serves only my dog's purposes; but my own brain labours at a knowledge which does nothing for me personally but make my body bitter to me and my decay and death a calamity. Were I not possessed with a purpose beyond my own I had better be a ploughman than a philosopher; for the ploughman lives as long as the philosopher, eats more, sleeps better, and rejoices in the wife of his bosom with less misgiving. This is because the philosopher is in the grip of the Life Force. This Life Force says to him 'I have done a thousand wonderful things unconsciously by merely willing to live and following the line of least resistance: now I want to know myself and my destination, and choose my path; so I have made a special brain – a philosopher's brain – to grasp this knowledge for me as the husbandman's hand grasps the plough for me. And this' says the Life Force to the philosopher 'must thou strive to do for me until thou diest, when I will make another brain and another philosopher to carry on the work.'

THE DEVIL. What is the use of knowing?

DON JUAN. Why, to be able to choose the line of greatest advantage instead of yielding in the direction of the least resistance. Does a ship sail to its destination no better than a log drifts nowhither? The philosopher is Nature's pilot. And there you have our difference: to be in hell is to drift: to be in heaven is to steer.

THE DEVIL. On the rocks, most likely.

DON JUAN. Pooh! which ship goes oftenest on the rocks or to the bottom? the drifting ship or the ship with a pilot on board?

THE DEVIL. Well, well, go your way, Señor Don Juan. I prefer to be my own master and not the tool of any blundering universal force. I know that beauty is good to look at; that music is good to hear; that love is good to feel; and that they are all good to think about and talk about. I know that to be well exercised in these sensations, emotions, and studies is to be a refined and cultivated being. Whatever they may say of me in churches on earth, I know that it is universally admitted in good society that the Prince of Darkness is a gentleman; and that is enough for me. As to your Life Force, which you think irresistible, it is the most resistible thing in the world for a person of any character.

But if you are naturally vulgar and credulous, as all re-
formers are, it will thrust you first into religion, where you
will sprinkle water on babies to save their souls from me;
then it will drive you from religion into science, where you
will snatch the babies from the water sprinkling and inocu-
late them with disease to save them from catching it
accidentally; then you will take to politics, where you will
become the catspaw of corrupt functionaries and the hench-
man of ambitious humbugs; and the end will be despair
and decrepitude, broken nerve and shattered hopes, vain
regrets for that worst and silliest of wastes and sacrifices, the
waste and sacrifice of the power of enjoyment: in a word,
the punishment of the fool who pursues the better before he
has secured the good.

DON JUAN. But at least I shall not be bored. The service of
the Life Force has that advantage, at all events. So fare you
well, Señor Satan.

THE DEVIL [*amiably*] Fare you well, Don Juan. I shall
often think of our interesting chats about things in general.
I wish you every happiness: heaven, as I said before, suits
some people. But if you should change your mind, do not
forget that the gates are always open here to the repentant
prodigal. If you feel at any time that warmth of heart, sincere unforced affection, innocent enjoyment, and warm,
breathing, palpitating reality –

DON JUAN. Why not say flesh and blood at once, though
we have left those two greasy commonplaces behind us?

THE DEVIL [*angrily*] You throw my friendly farewell back
in my teeth, then, Don Juan?

DON JUAN. By no means. But though there is much to be
learnt from a cynical devil, I really cannot stand a sentimental one.

[1901–1903]

John Bull's Other Island

From the beginning Shaw provoked laughter, and he always had ambivalent feelings about it. 'I have an incorrigible propensity for preaching,' he told the Church and Stage Guild in 1889. 'In conversation this did not make me so unpopular as might have been expected; for I have some unconscious and unintentional infirmity of expression which often leads people to doubt whether I am serious in my sermons.'[1] Nevertheless Shaw enjoyed laughter, and learned how to turn his 'infirmity' to good account. By 1906 he was lamenting the absence of laughter in the Christian Church:

> Unfortunately this Christian Church, founded gaily with a pun, has become the Church where you must not laugh; and so it is giving way to that older and greater Church to which I belong: the Church where the oftener you laugh the better, because by laughter only can you destroy evil without malice, and affirm good fellowship without mawkishness.[2]

The character of Peter Keegan, the defrocked Irish Catholic priest in *John Bull's Other Island*, emerged as one of the most sobering revelations of Shaw's own

[1] Dan H. Laurence, ed., *Platform and Pulpit* (Hart-Davis, 1962), p. 20.
[2] *Our Theatres in the Nineties*, Vol. I (Constable, 1932), p. vi.

34

existential pain. Even the comedic fatuousness of Tom Broadbent cannot break the spell of Keegan's despair.

LARRY. Are you really mad, Mr Keegan?

AUNT JUDY [*shocked*] Oh, Larry, how could you ask him such a thing?

LARRY. I dont think Mr Keegan minds. [*To Keegan*] What's the true version of the story of that black man you confessed on his deathbed?

KEEGAN. What story have you heard about that?

LARRY. I am informed that when the devil came for the black heathen, he took off your head and turned it three times round before putting it on again; and that your head's been turned ever since.

NORA [*reproachfully*] Larry!

KEEGAN [*blandly*] That is not quite what occurred. [*He collects himself for a serious utterance: they attend involuntarily.*] I heard that a black man was dying, and that the people were afraid to go near him. When I went to the place I found an elderly Hindoo, who told me one of those tales of unmerited misfortune, of cruel ill luck, of relentless persecution by destiny, which sometimes wither the commonplaces of consolation on the lips of a priest. But this man did not complain of his misfortunes. They were brought upon him, he said, by sins committed in a former existence. Then without a word of comfort from me, he died with a clear-eyed resignation that my most earnest exhortations have rarely produced in a Christian, and left me sitting there by his bedside with the mystery of this world suddenly revealed to me.

BROADBENT. That is a remarkable tribute to the liberty of conscience enjoyed by the subjects of our Indian Empire.

LARRY. No doubt; but may we venture to ask what is the mystery of this world?

KEEGAN. This world, sir, is very clearly a place of torment and penance, a place where the fool flourishes and the good and wise are hated and persecuted, a place where men and women torture one another in the name of love; where children are scourged and enslaved in the name of parental duty and education; where the weak in body are poisoned and mutilated in the name of healing, and the weak in character are put to the horrible torture of imprisonment, not for hours but for years, in the name of justice. It is a place where the hardest toil is a welcome refuge from the horror and tedium of pleasure, and where charity and good works are done only for hire to ransom the souls of the spoiler and the sybarite. Now, sir, there is only one place of horror and torment known to my religion; and that place is hell. Therefore it is plain to me that this earth of ours must be hell, and that we are all here, as the Indian revealed to me – perhaps he was sent to reveal it to me – to expiate crimes committed by us in a former existence.

*　　　*　　　*

KEEGAN. Sir: when you speak to me of English and Irish you forget that I am a Catholic. My country is not Ireland nor England, but the whole mighty realm of my Church. For me there are but two countries: heaven and hell; but two conditions of men: salvation and damnation. Standing here between you the Englishman, so clever in your foolishness, and this Irishman, so foolish in his cleverness, I cannot in my ignorance be sure which of you is the more deeply damned; but I should be unfaithful to my calling if I opened the gates of my heart less widely to one than to the other.

LARRY. In either case it would be an impertinence, Mr Keegan, as your approval is not of the slightest consequence to us. What use do you suppose all this drivel is to men with serious practical business in hand?

BROADBENT. I dont agree with that, Larry. I think these things cannot be said too often: they keep up the moral tone of the community. As you know, I claim the right to think for myself in religious matters: in fact, I am ready to avow myself a bit of a – of a – well, I dont care who knows it – a bit of a Unitarian; but if the Church of England contained a few men like Mr Keegan, I should certainly join it.

KEEGAN. You do me too much honour, sir. [*With priestly humility to Larry*] Mr Doyle: I am to blame for having unintentionally set your mind somewhat on edge against me. I beg your pardon.

LARRY [*unimpressed and hostile*] I didnt stand on ceremony with you: you neednt stand on it with me. Fine manners and fine words are cheap in Ireland: you can keep both for my friend here, who is still imposed on by them. *I* know their value.

KEEGAN. You mean you dont know their value.

LARRY [*angrily*] I mean what I say.

KEEGAN [*turning quietly to the Englishman*] You see, Mr Broadbent, I only make the hearts of my countrymen harder when I preach to them: the gates of hell still prevail against me. I shall wish you good evening. I am better alone, at the Round Tower, dreaming of heaven. [*He goes up the hill.*]

LARRY. Aye, thats it! there you are! dreaming! dreaming! dreaming! dreaming!

KEEGAN [*halting and turning to them for the last time*] Every dream is a prophecy: every jest is an earnest in the womb of Time.

BROADBENT [*reflectively*] Once, when I was a small kid, I dreamt I was in heaven. [*They both stare at him.*] It was a sort of pale blue satin place, with all the pious old ladies in our congregation sitting as if they were at a service; and

37

there was some awful person in the study at the other side of the hall. I didnt enjoy it, you know. What is it like in your dreams?

KEEGAN. In my dreams it is a country where the State is the Church and the Church the people: three in one and one in three. It is a commonwealth in which work is play and play is life: three in one and one in three. It is a temple in which the priest is the worshipper and the worshipper the worshipped: three in one and one in three. It is a godhead in which all life is human and all humanity divine: three in one and one in three. It is, in short, the dream of a madman. [*He goes away across the hill.*]

[1904]

Major Barbara

Shaw would never accept the kind of pragmatism that declares whatever works is right. His mysticism, none the less, had a pragmatic flavour. 'If a man cannot look evil in the face without illusion, he will never know what it really is, or combat it effectually', he wrote in the Preface to *Major Barbara*. There is no point in a religion that will not face the facts of our world.

Major Barbara, despite its relatively high popularity, is often described as an unsatisfactory play, because the munitions maker, Undershaft, is clearly the victor over Barbara's salvationist religion and, in fact, destroys it. But Undershaft is himself a mystic, and the new faith he catalyses in Barbara is higher than the one she abandons, even though it gives her no easy answers to the great human problems of poverty and war. The world is not yet ready to take up her vision of doing God's will for its own sake.

BARBARA. Oh, if only I could get away from you and from father and from it all! if I could have the wings of a dove and fly away to heaven!

CUSINS. And leave me!

BARBARA. Yes, you, and all the other naughty mischievous children of men. But I cant. I was happy in the Salvation

Army for a moment. I escaped from the world into a paradise of enthusiasm and prayer and soul saving; but the moment our money ran short, it all came back to Bodger: it was he who saved our people: he, and the Prince of Darkness, my papa. Undershaft and Bodger: their hands stretch everywhere: when we feed a starving fellow creature, it is with their bread, because there is no other bread; when we tend the sick, it is in the hospitals they endow; if we turn from the churches they build, we must kneel on the stones of the streets they pave. As long as that lasts, there is no getting away from them. Turning our backs on Bodger and Undershaft is turning our backs on life.

CUSINS. I thought you were determined to turn your back on the wicked side of life.

BARBARA. There is no wicked side: life is all one. And I never wanted to shirk my share in whatever evil must be endured, whether it be sin or suffering. I wish I could cure you of middle-class ideas, Dolly.

CUSINS [*gasping*] Middle cl—! A snub! A social snub to me! from the daughter of a foundling!

BARBARA. That is why I have no class, Dolly: I come straight out of the heart of the whole people. If I were middle-class I should turn my back on my father's business; and we should both live in an artistic drawing-room, with you reading the reviews in one corner, and I in the other at the piano, playing Schumann: both very superior persons, and neither of us a bit of use. Sooner than that, I would sweep out the guncotton shed, or be one of Bodger's barmaids. Do you know what would have happened if you had refused papa's offer?

CUSINS. I wonder!

BARBARA. I should have given you up and married the man who accepted it. After all, my dear old mother has more sense than any of you. I felt like her when I saw this

MAJOR BARBARA

place – felt that I must have it – that never, never, never could I let it go; only she thought it was the houses and the kitchen ranges and the linen and china, when it was really all the human souls to be saved: not weak souls in starved bodies, sobbing with gratitude for a scrap of bread and treacle, but fullfed, quarrelsome, snobbish, uppish creatures, all standing on their little rights and dignities, and thinking that my father ought to be greatly obliged to them for making so much money for him – and so he ought. That is where salvation is really wanted. My father shall never throw it in my teeth again that my converts were bribed with bread. [*She is transfigured.*] I have got rid of the bribe of bread. I have got rid of the bribe of heaven. Let God's work be done for its own sake: the work he had to create us to do because it cannot be done except by living men and women. When I die, let him be in my debt, not I in his; and let me forgive him as becomes a woman of my rank.

CUSINS. Then the way of life lies through the factory of death?

BARBARA. Yes, through the raising of hell to heaven and of man to God, through the unveiling of an eternal light in the Valley of The Shadow. [*Seizing him with both hands*] Oh, did you think my courage would never come back? did you believe that I was a deserter? that I, who have stood in the streets, and taken my people to my heart, and talked of the holiest and greatest things with them, could ever turn back and chatter foolishly to fashionable people about nothing in a drawing room? Never, never, never, never: Major Barbara will die with the colours. Oh! and I have my dear little Dolly boy still; and he has found me my place and my work. Glory Hallelujah! [*She kisses him*].

CUSINS. My dearest: consider my delicate health. I cannot stand as much happiness as you can.

[1905]

41

On Miracles: A Retort

Shaw enjoyed debating with his friendly opponent, G. K. Chesterton, especially on religious matters. Chesterton was to publish the first book-length study of Shaw the year following this exchange about miracles, and some years later was to become a convert to Catholicism.

As Chesterton's elder by eighteen years, Shaw chides him for not having been part of the Secularist debates of the 70s and 80s, the heyday of the National Secular Society, the Positivists, and the free-thinking congregations, all of which fostered the turbulent atmosphere into which Shaw stepped when he arrived from Dublin in 1876. The boisterous lecture halls were a part of his own higher education.

It is interesting to compare these journalistic comments with his more considered views on Joan's voices in 1924.

In the course of his encounter with Mr Belfort Bax, Mr Chesterton takes the opportunity to tread on the tail of my coat. Lest the humorous ingenuity of the attack should be lost on the careless reader, let me quote it. 'Ask Bernard Shaw,' says Mr Chesterton, 'to speak on any other subject, and he explodes with epigrammatic sagacity: ask him why he denies miracles, and his answer is a curious and dreary compound of a Hyde Park Secularist and a Broad Church

Bishop.' The humour of this lies in the fact that nobody ever asks me why I deny miracles, because I never do deny them, but, on the contrary, spend my life largely affirming them. And I do not see why a compound of a Hyde Park Secularist and a Broad Church Bishop need be dreary or even curious: the Victorian Broad Church Bishops who had a dash of the Hyde Park Secularist in them were particularly lively Bishops; and the combination has not become conventional, though I quite agree that the type is obsolescing. But I have never in my life heard either a Broad Church Bishop or a Hyde Park Secularist put forward my view of miracles. I will now proceed to lay down the law on the subject of miracles; and I defy Mr Chesterton to braze his cheerful countenance to the extremity of telling me that it is a relic of that Victorian past which he imagines, but which I remember.

The world is full of miracles. Consciousness, for instance, is a complete miracle. Birth is a miracle; life is a miracle; and death was a miracle until quite recently, when Weismann made out a very plausible case for regarding it as a rather late product of natural selection. Anyhow, there are lots of miracles about; and the man who denies their existence is always a man who is simply wrong in his definition of a miracle. By a miracle he means only something that he is not accustomed to and did not expect.

Miracles can be divided into two main classes: (1) Miraculous events as to the actual occurrence of which there is no question and no doubt. (2) Miraculous events of which the occurrence is not generally admitted. For instance, it is alleged of a certain Lazarus that he achieved the miracle of living; and nobody doubts or denies this. It is further alleged that Lazarus rose from the dead at the command of Jesus. Though this was a very much simpler feat than to get born and up, yet nobody believes that

he actually did it except people who would believe anything.

The reason of this is obvious enough. None of us has ever
seen a man raised from the dead except on the banks of the
Serpentine by a policeman skilled in the art of inducing
artificial respiration; and even this exception we try to get
out of by the manifestly futile contention that the resurrected
one was not dead – that he was only drowned. Still, the
distinction between a familiar miracle and an unprecedented
one accounts roughly for a good deal of the fact that we are
credulous as to some miracles and incredulous as to others.
But it does not account for all of it. There are certain kinds
of miracles that so please our imaginations or promise us
relief or profit of some sort that we believe them in spite of
experience. Doctors, like witches, profess to perform all the
miracles attributed to founders of religions; and though
they fail daily, people are actually sent to prison for doubting such professions.

Finally, one observes that the moment you get beyond
the range of those miracles which everybody has seen performed often enough to have lost all sense of their being
miracles, credulity and incredulity are entirely tempera-
mental and dogmatic. It was my grasp of this fact that
enabled me to deflate Mr Chesterton recently at Clifford's
Inn. Like the old-fashioned Secularist, he started arguing
about miracles. He argued, in effect, that it is ridiculous for
us, gorged as we are daily by unquestionable miracles, to
make a difficulty about believing in this or that event merely
because it is a miracle. And he was quite right. If you believe
that the sun will rise tomorrow morning, you give up all
right to deny that I can turn a dog into a cat merely on the
ground that such a metamorphosis is a miracle. But that
does not alter the fact that everybody believes that the sun
will rise tomorrow, and that nobody believes that I can turn

44

a dog into a cat. I quite grant that the Victorian Secularist who tries to make out that the one event is a miracle and the other is not, can be controversially spifflicated by Mr Chesterton, who is nevertheless not a bit more credulous than Tyndall or Leslie Stephen. But Mr Chesterton, over-shooting his conclusion with his usual impetuosity, not only devastated the gasping Rationalists and Materialists in the audience by demonstrating this, but went on to imply that since he might as well be hanged for a sheep as for a lamb, he was prepared to swallow all the miracles of religious legend, holding himself up as one who had risen into a mystic sphere in which vulgar incredulity as to miracles had fallen off him as a garment.

I ruined this transfiguration in a very simple manner. I am by this time a sufficiently good judge of men to be able to guess the place at which they will draw the line between their dogmatic credulity and their dogmatic incredulity. I took a particular miracle, one just as well vouched for as any other particular miracle, and not a bit more miraculous than dozens of miracles in which Mr Chesterton and I believe, but one in which, nevertheless, I dogmatically do not believe and in which I knew that Mr Chesterton did not believe. I asked him did he believe in that miracle. He could easily have floored me by telling a direct lie and saying he did. But it was miraculously impossible for him to do so, as I knew it would be. He made a gallant attempt to shake my teeth out of his calf, so to speak, by saying that there were just as good reasons for his believing in this particular miracle as for his believing in many other things which I and everybody else in the room believe in as well. But I knew too much about miracles to be shaken off. I kept repeating, both when I was in order and out of order, the flat question as to whether he believed or did not believe in that particular miracle. He could not say that he believed in

45

it. Nobody believed in it. Nobody believed that he could believe in it. And the impression produced was – most unfairly and erroneously – that Mr Chesterton's argument had fallen to pieces.

A point to be observed about miracles is that mankind may be divided into people who, like Hume, consider that any 'natural' explanation of an event is to be preferred to the no-explanation that it is miraculous, and the other sort of people who have the opposite preference, and think it much more likely that the spirit of their late grandmother is rapping on the table than that I am tapping my boot against the leg of my chair, as I generally am on such occasions. These marvellors will not believe in a religion unless its apostles entertain them with conjuring tricks: the other sort will not believe in religion at all because concessions have been made by all religions to the other party. And of course these two sorts of people are mostly the same sort. Professor Tyndall would not believe in spontaneous generation on any terms; but he made no bones about attributing to every atom a positive and negative magnetic pole, and a consequent self-arrangement of atoms into crystals, and mountains, and sunsets, and vertebrate animals, stopping short quite unaccountably of cherubim and seraphim, who, if they exist, may surely be as atomic and magnetic as anybody else. Other learned doctors are quite ready to believe that when St Paul's head was chopped off it bounded away, leaving a new spring of fresh water to mark the place of each ricochet; but they will not believe the simplest fact of natural history discovered by Darwin.

Let us confess, then, that the man who argues that miracles must be either credible or incredible, and that if some miracles are credible (as they undoubtedly are), then all miracles must be credible, is the most hopelessly unreal kind of logician. The plain facts are that some miracles are

credible and some are incredible, and that every different
sort of man draws the line in a different place. Therefore
there is nothing to be got out of miracles, either one way or
the other, by special pleaders for or against any particular
religion.

Further, it is inevitable that a man's quality shall be
judged by the situation of the boundary between his
credulity and his incredulity. We cannot help saying, concerning any given miracle, either 'the man who believes this
would believe anything', meaning, 'the man who believes
this must be a silly fool', or 'the man who will not believe
this will not believe anything', meaning, 'the man who cannot feel the truth of this must be a damned fool'. (Need I
say that I am using the word damned literally and not
abusively?) But these sayings are inevitable only because it
is inevitable that men should express their opinions. Each
miracle remains a separate matter of opinion after all; and
every brace of miracles is like the two women grinding in
the field: one shall be taken and the other left by that
capricious human appetite which we call faith. When I was
taken to the pantomime at a very early age, I believed
piously in the fairy queen and ecstatically in the clown; but
I did not believe in the clown *because* I believed in the fairy
queen, nor would I have forsaken her if I had found the
clown out. I no longer believe in either of them in that
particular way. And these are not the only opinions I have
changed. I have gained beliefs and lost beliefs; but I never
took on a new belief merely because I already entertained
beliefs just as incredible; and I never threw off a belief
merely because I had already thrown off others just as
credible. That is not the way the human imagination works.

Such is my position about miracles. I offer it as completely up-to-date, although it was probably held by Adam,
or would have been if Adam had had my opportunities of

observation. And I challenge Mr Chesterton to name any Victorian Secularist or Broad Church Bishop who anticipated me in it. Not that it would be any the worse for having been so anticipated; but, as a matter of fact, both Secularists and Broad Church Bishops always struck me as resolutely blinding themselves to it because they had jumped to the conclusion that you could not discredit any miracle without discrediting all miracles, and that if you admitted the possibility of one miracle, you were bound to swallow all the rest, not noticing, apparently, that whether you were bound to or not, you just didnt.

[1908]

The Shewing-Up of Blanco Posnet

Although the Life Force, unlike the conventional concept of God, is not omnipotent, it occasionally invades the conscience of a most unlikely agent and compels him to do its will. The 'inspired' character is familiar enough in Shaw's plays to be expected.

One of his strangest works is the short 'American Western' dealing with the apprehension and trial of a horse-thief. The opening directions of *The Shewing-Up of Blanco Posnet* call for dress and speech 'of pioneers of civilization in a territory of the United States of America', but no Western American ever said 'Bully for you', or 'Not likely', or 'I shan't blab' (to mean 'I won't squeal'). It is nevertheless a lively and amusing play, and it ends with the disreputable horse-thief, heretofore proud of his wickedness, humbly confessing that he went soft and risked his own life by giving the stolen horse to save an unknown woman's child.

There is no explanation for this conduct except that God 'plays cat and mouse with you. He lets you run loose until you think you're shut of him; and when you least expect it he's got you.' Under the circumstances Blanco Posnet, acquitted, feels called upon to preach the following sermon.

BLANCO. Dearly beloved brethren—

A BOY. Same to you, Blanco. [*Laughter.*]

BLANCO. And many of them. Boys: this is a rotten world.

ANOTHER BOY. Lord have mercy on us, miserable sinners. [*More laughter.*]

BLANCO [*Forcibly*] No: thats where youre wrong. Dont flatter yourselves that youre miserable sinners. Am I a miserable sinner? No: I'm a fraud and a failure. I started in to be a bad man like the rest of you. You all started in to be bad men or you wouldnt be in this jumped-up, jerked-off, hospital-turned-out camp that calls itself a town. I took the broad path because I thought I was a man and not a snivelling canting turning-the-other-cheek apprentice angel serving his time in a vale of tears. They talked Christianity to us on Sundays; but when they really meant business they told us never to take a blow without giving it back, and to get dollars. When they talked the golden rule to me, I just looked at them as if they werent there, and spat. But when they told me to try to live my life so that I could always look my fellowman straight in the eye and tell him to go to hell, that fetched me.

THE BOYS. Quite right. Good. Bully for you, Blanco, old son. Right good sense too. Aha-a-ah!

BLANCO. Yes; but whats come of it all? Am I a real bad man? a man of game and grit? a man that does what he likes and goes over or through other people to his own gain? or am I a snivelling cry-baby that let a horse his life depended on be took from him by a woman, and then sat on the grass looking at the rainbow and let himself be took like a hare in a trap by Strapper Kemp: a lad whose back I or any grown man here could break against his knee? I'm a rottener fraud and failure than the Elder here. And you're all as rotten as me, or youd have lynched me.

A BOY. Anything to oblige you, Blanco.

ANOTHER. We can do it yet if you feel really bad about it.

BLANCO. No: the devil's gone out of you. We're all frauds. Theres none of us real good and none of us real bad.

ELDER DANIELS. There is One above, Blanco.

BLANCO. What do you know about Him? you that always talk as if He never did anything without asking your rotten leave first? Why did the child die? Tell me that if you can. He cant have wanted to kill the child. Why did He make me go soft on the child if He was going hard on it Himself? Why should He go hard on the innocent kid and go soft on a rotten thing like me? Why did I go soft myself? Why did the Sheriff go soft? Why did Feemy go soft? Whats this game that upsets our game? For seems to me theres two games bein played. Our game is a rotten game that makes me feel I'm dirt and that youre all as rotten dirt as me. T'other game may be a silly game; but it aint rotten. When the Sheriff played it he stopped being rotten. When Feemy played it the paint nearly dropped off her face. When I played it I cursed myself for a fool; but I lost the rotten feel all the same.

ELDER DANIELS. It was the Lord speaking to your soul, Blanco.

BLANCO. Oh yes: you know all about the Lord, dont you? Youre in the Lord's confidence. He wouldnt for the world do anything to shock you, would He, Boozy dear? Yah! What about the croup? It was early days when He made the croup, I guess. It was the best He could think of then; but when it turned out wrong on His hands He made you and me to fight the croup for Him. You bet He didnt make us for nothing; and He wouldnt have made us at all if He could have done His work without us. By Gum, that must be what we're for! He'd never have made us to be rotten drunken blackguards like me, and good-for-nothing rips like Feemy. He made me because He had a job for me. He let

51

me run loose til the job was ready; and then I had to come along and do it, hanging or no hanging. And I tell you it didnt feel rotten: it felt bully, just bully. Anyhow, I got the rotten feel off me for a minute of my life; and I'll go through fire to get it off me again. Look here! which of you will marry Feemy Evans?

THE BOYS [*uproariously*] Who speaks first? Who'll marry Feemy? Come along, Jack. Nows your chance, Peter. Pass along a husband for Feemy. Oh my! Feemy!

FEEMY [*shortly*] Keep your tongue off me, will you?

BLANCO. Feemy was a rose of the broad path, wasnt she? You all thought her the champion bad woman of this district. Well, she's a failure as a bad woman; and I'm a failure as a bad man. So let Brother Daniels marry us to keep all the rottenness in the family. What do you say, Feemy?

FEEMY. Thank you; but when I marry I'll marry a man that could do a decent action without surprising himself out of his senses. Youre like a child with a new toy: you and your bit of human kindness!

THE WOMAN. How many would have done it with their life at stake?

FEEMY. Oh well, if youre so much taken with him, marry him yourself. Youd be what people call a good wife to him, wouldnt you?

THE WOMAN. I was a good wife to the child's father. I dont think any woman wants to be a good wife twice in her life. I want somebody to be a good husband to me now.

BLANCO. Any offer, gentlemen, on that understanding? [*The boys shake their heads.*] Oh, it's a rotten game, our game. Heres a real good woman; and she's had enough of it, finding that it only led to being put upon.

HANNAH. Well, if there was nothing wrong in the world there wouldnt be anything left for us to do, would there?

ELDER DANIELS. Be of good cheer, brothers. Seek the path.

52

BLANCO. No. No more paths. No more broad and narrow. No more good and bad. Theres no good and bad; but by Jiminy, gents, theres a rotten game, and theres a great game. I played the rotten game; but the great game was played on me; and now I'm for the great game every time. Amen. Gentlemen: let us adjourn to the saloon. I stand the drinks. [*He jumps down from the table.*]

THE BOYS. Right you are, Blanco. Drinks round. Come along, boys. Blanco's standing. Right along to the Elder's. Hurrah! [*They rush out, dragging the Elder with them.*]

BLANCO [*to Feemy, offering his hand*] Shake, Feemy.

FEEMY. Get along, you blackguard.

BLANCO. It's come over me again, same as when the kid touched me, same as when you swore a lie to save my neck.

FEEMY. Oh well, here. [*They shake hands.*]

[1909]

God must be Non-Sectarian and International

Reginald John Campbell, ethereal and poetic, was the Congregationalist pastor of City Temple from 1902 to 1915. He inspired the fiercest loyalties and the wildest attacks, and drew the largest congregations in the memory of any London church-goer. He was a modernist in his reading of the Scriptures and precipitated a nation-wide debate on *The New Theology* with his best-selling book in 1907. He was also an avowed Socialist, a warm supporter of Keir Hardie.

Shaw and Campbell were on the most friendly of terms until Campbell abandoned Nonconformity in the midst of the war, recanted his New Theology, and became an Anglican priest. During his incumbency at City Temple he invited Shaw to speak at midweek gatherings a number of times. *The Christian Commonwealth*, unofficially an organ of the Temple, devoted many columns to Shaw's utterances. The *Commonwealth*, however, tended to emphasize Shaw's agreement with the pastor rather than his occasional disagreement, and the following letter was written to correct any misapprehension that Shaw, even when speaking from a church pulpit, could accept Campbell's most liberal concept of a Christian God.

The difference between Mr R. J. Campbell's position and mine is really part of the fact that we have a different job, and that the theology that suffices for his job will not suffice for mine. Mr Campbell, as pastor of the Christian congregation of the City Temple, knows that Christianity is a first necessity of spiritual life for its members, because to them no spiritual life is intelligible except in terms of Christianity. But my congregation is as wide as the English language, and, indeed, wider. It includes Jews, Mohammedans, Agnostics, and all sorts of non-Christians with whom the first condition of an acceptable theology, or biology, or psychology, or whatever they call it (for I am not free even to use the word theology) is that it shall be entirely independent of Christianity. If I were to write about Jesus as Mr Campbell does, and pray to him, I should presently be up against a Jewish reader who would say to me: 'My good sir, all this is no use to me. I see nothing in this man Jesus but a seditious carpenter whom my people executed, very properly in my opinion, exactly as your Christians executed Savonarola and John of Leyden, because he was upsetting all law and order without having any clear or practicable idea of what to put in their place. Your Mr Campbell is simply an idolator; and, though he may find that his idolatry is a convenient instrument for saving the souls of congregations of Christians who have been taught from their earliest childhood to associate all their highest idealism with the personality of Jesus, I and my co-religionists have not been trained in that way; we crucified Jesus, and have never recanted that very practical criticism of him; so if you wish to draw us into your communion you must not ask us to rate Jesus higher generically than any other historical character. You must even be content to find that many of us consider that we are making too great a concession in admitting that Jesus was a

55

historical person, and not a mere excuse for robbing, out-lawing, and murdering the chosen people.' On which some good Moslem will cry: 'I do not at all agree with our Israelite friend about Jesus. He was a very worthy prophet, and to some extent the forerunner of The Prophet, who spoke very handsomely of him. But you will surely not con-test the enormous superiority of Mahomet. Jesus, as your most enthusiastic Christian, Mr Campbell, admits, preached to a highly civilized people a gospel which had been propa-gated among them for several hundred years. But he was incapable of organization, and so timid and helpless person-ally that he was defeated by a second-rate high priest, and beaten and executed. Mahomet preached God to hordes of fierce idolators who worshipped stones. He began with two followers: his wife and a boy of sixteen; and he ended on one of the greatest temporal and spiritual thrones the world has ever seen, having not only taught the people, but fought for them and conquered for them, and put the Caiaphases and Pilates of Arabia under his feet.' And yet a third critic will come and say: 'Really, Mr Shaw, I am surprised to find you pretending to listen respectfully to these two imbeciles, one of them worshipping an Arab camel driver who divided the year into lunar months and thought the mountains were weights to keep the earth from being blown away, and the other prating about his wretched tribe being the chosen people of a long since demolished idol. Pray, have you ever heard of modern science? Have you ever heard of Evolution? Do you really believe? does any-body worth counting really believe? in the Resurrection, in a sky rocket Ascension, in the commercial theory of the Atonement, in the Garden of Eden, and the miracles, and all the rest of it? Do you expect me to associate myself with a propaganda that gives the slightest countenance to these absurdities for the sake of conciliating ignorant labourers

56

and petty tradesmen and the priestly exploiters of their credulity?' And so on, and so forth.

What am I to say to these people? They are all as right as Mr Campbell: that is, they feel exactly as they say. Some of the ablest of our young musicians and writers tell me that they find Beethoven's harmony intolerably uninteresting, and that they cannot read Dickens. Well, they are none the less entitled to their sensations because I am saturated with Dickens and Beethoven. Evidently, if I am to work with them at all, I must take care not to make my views on music and literature hinge on an adoration of Beethoven and Dickens. But for the purposes of a Beethoven society or a Dickens Fellowship I might safely disregard them, and do very good work by appealing to the love of Beethoven and Dickens. Just so can Mr Campbell do good work by appealing to the love of Jesus felt by the congregation of the City Temple. But this very thing that helps him so powerfully would be fatal to me.

For the same reason I must not talk about 'The Father'. If I do, my friend Blatchford will promptly say: 'Let us understand one another, Shaw. A father is evidently a mature person of the male sex. That is the beginning of definiteness. Let us follow up that beginning. If we are looking for a person, and a male person, let us inform the police. They will want to know his age, his height, the colour of his hair and eyes, the place where he was last seen and who saw him, his customary habits and resorts, his race, colour, and language, and any other information that may lead to his identification, and, if necessary, arrest.' At the City Temple it is easy to dispose of all this by crying 'Throw the blasphemer out' and throwing him out. But the great majority of the subjects of the British Empire (do not forget the East) would laugh quite good-humouredly and consider that Mr Blatchford had reduced 'The Father' to

57

absurdity very successfully, wittily, and properly. I cannot unite even the sexes on a male Life Force; and as to uniting the nations on a black or white or yellow one (I should like to see the City Temple congregation confronted with a picture of the Trinity represented as a German, a negro, and a Chinaman), such an idolization is hopeless. I repeat, a combination of a white Father and a white Madonna may serve very well for the purpose of European Christian congregations. But for my purpose, which is to find a common faith for Mr Campbell and Mr Blatchford – both obviously good men, who should be helping instead of hindering one another – 'The Father' is out of the question.

I really cannot accept Mr Campbell's apology for the crucifixion. If I were a deity, and anyone made such a plainly desperate attempt to whitewash me I should throw thunderbolts. The crucifixion manifested nothing but the cruelty and bigotry of the high priest and his supporters, and the impotence of imperial power and culture face to face with cruelty and bigotry. Mr Campbell's view seems to imply that if there had been a little more cruelty the effect would have been still more complete. As a matter of fact many more horrible executions are on record. John of Leyden was so hideously tortured to death at Munster that the wretched Christian bishop who had to preside over the execution went home and died of horror. The torture and execution of Gliebof by Peter the Great was much more horrible than the crucifixion; and even Gliebof's fate was less horrible than that of several of the women on whom Peter wreaked his vengeance. We are ourselves responsible for the executions at Denshawai, which were less defensible politically than the execution of Jesus, and were, relatively to our customs and the morality we profess, much more deliberately wicked and cruel. Mr Campbell's apology applies to all those horrors just as much as to the crucifixion.

He will admit this, and repeat that Omnipotence could manifest its benevolence in no other way. But if he really means Omnipotence, he must write would instead of could; and that change turns his Omnipotent into 'the almighty fiend' of Shelley.

I do not deny that the intentions of the Life Force have been good all through; and therefore Mr Campbell may say that all the good it has done was intended from the beginning. But he says also that all the bad it has done (and I have just cited some sensational examples) was intended from the beginning. That is not quite so cheering. I know only one method of finding out how to do anything. It is the method of Trial and Error. If the City Temple maintains that the Life Force intended its errors, it will not be long before not one stone of it shall be left on another; for this is the doctrine that killed religion in the nineteenth century, and may bury it in the twentieth if we do not root it out.

Finally, may I say that my mind is so constituted that if I could conceive a god as deliberately creating something less than himself, I should class him as a cad. If he were simply satisfied with himself, I should class him as a lazy coxcomb. *My* god must continually strive to surpass himself.

[1912]

59

Common Sense About the War

Shaw was not wholly a pacifist, at least not at the time the First World War burst upon Europe. But the stupidity and the hypocrisy of the diplomatic fumbling which led to the holocaust infuriated him as no other series of man's foibles in his entire lifetime.

His first outburst, *Common Sense About the War*, earned him the epithet of Most Hated Man in England. However his republication of *What I Really Wrote About the War* found, by 1932, a more chastened public granting the validity of most of his wartime insight.

Shaw was particularly bitter about the abject failure of the Churches to maintain any shred of Jesus's peace testimony.

And now, where in our society is the organ whose function it should be to keep us constantly in mind that, as Lassalle said, 'the sword is never right', and to shudder with him at the fact that 'the Lie is a European Power'? In no previous war have we struck that top note of keen irony, the closing of the Stock Exchange and not of the Church. The pagans were more logical: they closed the Temple of Peace when they drew the sword. We turn our Temples of Peace promptly into temples of war, and exhibit our parsons as the most pugnacious characters in the community. I venture to affirm that the sense of scandal given by this is far deeper and more general than the Church thinks, especially among the working classes, who are apt either to take religion seriously or else to repudiate it and criticize it closely. When a bishop at the first shot abandons the worship of Christ and rallies his flock round the altar of Mars, he may be acting patriotically, necessarily, manfully, rightly; but that does not justify him in pretending that there has been no change, and that Christ is, in effect, Mars. The straightforward course, and the one that would serve the Church best in the long run, would be to close our professedly Christian Churches the moment war is declared by us, and reopen them only on the signing of the treaty of peace. No doubt to many of us the privation thus imposed would be far worse than the privation of small change, of horses and motor cars, of express trains, and all the other prosaic inconveniences of war. But would it be worse than the privation of faith, and the horror of the soul, wrought by the spectacle of nations praying to their common Father to assist them in sabring and bayoneting and blowing one another to pieces with explosives that are also corrosives, and of the Church organizing this monstrous paradox instead of protesting against it? Would it make less atheists or more? Atheism is not a simple homogeneous phenomenon. There is the youthful atheism with which every able modern mind begins: an atheism that clears the soul of superstitions and terrors and servilities and base compliances and hypocrisies, and lets in the light of heaven. And there is the atheism of despair and pessimism: the sullen cry with which so many of us at this moment, looking on blinded deafened maimed wrecks that were once able-bodied admirable lovable men, and on priests blessing war, and newspapers and statesmen and exempt old men hounding young men on to it, and saying, 'I know now there is no God'. What has the Church in its present

61

attitude to set against this crushed acceptance of darkness except the quaint but awful fact that there are cruder people on whom horrifying calamities have just the opposite effect, because they seem the work of some power so overwhelming in its malignity that it must be worshipped because it is mighty? Let the Church beware how it plays to that gallery. If all the Churches of Europe closed their doors until the drums ceased rolling they would act as a most powerful reminder that though the glory of war is a famous and ancient glory, it is not the final glory of God.

[1914]

On the Prospects of Christianity

In the play *Misalliance* Shaw has one of his breezier characters, John Tarleton, say:

> Whats the use of telling children to read the Bible when you know they wont? I was kept away from the Bible for forty years by being told to read it when I was young. Then I picked it up one evening in Sunderland when I had left all my papers in the train; and I found it wasnt half bad.

How literally this was Shaw's own story is hard to guess, but he did re-read the Bible as an adult and found it not half bad. His exegesis of the New Testament would not, perhaps, impress Bible scholars – they would find some obvious errors in his reading – but they might possibly envy his ability to respond at the same time with freshness and sophistication to a scripture which, for most of them, had accreted centuries of layers of association and interpretation that were all but impenetrable.

In his Preface to *Androcles and the Lion*, written in 1915, two years after the production of the play itself, Shaw reviews the set of books written by Matthew, Mark, Luke, and John, with some general comments 'On the Prospects of Christianity'. Only his remarks on Luke are included here.

Why not give Christianity a Trial?

The question seems a hopeless one after 2000 years of resolute adherence to the old cry of 'Not this man, but Barabbas'. Yet it is beginning to look as if Barabbas was a failure, in spite of his strong right hand, his victories, his empires, his millions of money, and his moralities and churches and political constitutions. 'This man' has not been a failure yet; for nobody has ever been sane enough to try his way. But he has had one quaint triumph. Barabbas has stolen his name and taken his cross as a standard. There is a sort of compliment in that. There is even a sort of loyalty in it, like that of the brigand who breaks every law and yet claims to be a patriotic subject of the king who makes them. We have always had a curious feeling that though we crucified Christ on a stick, he somehow managed to get hold of the right end of it, and that if we were better men we might try his plan.... I am no more a Christian than Pilate was, or you, gentle reader; and yet, like Pilate, I greatly prefer Jesus to Annas and Caiaphas; and I am ready to admit that after contemplating the world and human nature for nearly sixty years, I see no way out of the world's misery but the way which would have been found by Christ's will if he had undertaken the work of a modern practical statesman.

Pray do not at this early point lose patience with me and shut the book. I assure you I am as sceptical and scientific and modern a thinker as you will find anywhere. I grant you I know a great deal more about economics and politics than Jesus did, and can do things he could not do. I am by all Barabbasque standards a person of much better character and standing, and greater practical sense. I have no sympathy with vagabonds and talkers who try to reform society by taking men away from their regular productive work and making vagabonds and talkers of them too; and if I had been Pilate I should have recognized as plainly as he the necessity for suppressing attacks on the existing social order, however corrupt that order might be, by people with no knowledge of government and no power to construct political machinery to carry out their views, acting on the very dangerous delusion that the end of the world was at hand. I make no defence of such Christians as Savonarola and John of Leyden: they were scuttling the ship before they had learned how to build a raft; and it became necessary to throw them overboard to save the crew. I say this to set myself right with respectable society; but I must still insist that if Jesus could have worked out the practical problems of a Communist constitution, an admitted obligation to deal with crime without revenge or punishment, and a full assumption by humanity of divine responsibilities, he would have conferred an incalculable benefit on mankind, because these distinctive demands of his are now turning out to be good sense and sound economics.

I say distinctive, because his common humanity and his subjection to time and space (that is, to the Syrian life of his period) involved his belief in many things, true and false, that in no way distinguish him from other Syrians of that time. But such common beliefs do not constitute specific Christianity any more than wearing a beard, working in a carpenter's shop, or believing that the earth is flat and that the stars could drop on it from heaven like hailstones. Christianity interests practical statesmen now because of the doctrines that distinguished Christ from the Jews and the Barabbasques generally, including ourselves.

*   *   *

LUKE

Luke the Literary Artist

When we come to Luke, we come to a later story-teller, and one with a stronger natural gift for his art. Before you have read twenty lines of Luke's gospel you are aware that you have passed from the chronicler writing for the sake of recording important facts, to the artist, telling the story for the sake of telling it. At the very outset he achieves the most charming idyll in the Bible: the story of Mary crowded out of the inn into the stable and laying her newly-born son in the manger, and of the shepherds abiding in the field keeping watch over their flocks by night, and how the angel of the Lord came upon them, and the glory of the Lord shone around them, and suddenly there was with the angel a multitude of the heavenly host. These shepherds go to the stable and take the place of the kings in Matthew's chronicle. So completely has this story conquered and fascinated our imagination that most of us suppose all the gospels to contain it; but it is Luke's story and his alone: none of the others have the smallest hint of it.

The Charm of Luke's Narrative

Luke gives the charm of sentimental romance to every incident. The Annunciation, as described by Matthew, is made to Joseph, and is simply a warning to him not to divorce his wife for misconduct. In Luke's gospel it is made to Mary herself, at much greater length, with a sense of the ecstasy of the bride of the Holy Ghost. Jesus is refined and softened almost out of recognition: the stern peremptory disciple of John the Baptist, who never addresses a Pharisee or a Scribe without an insulting epithet, becomes a considerate, gentle, sociable, almost urbane person; and the

66

Chauvinist Jew becomes a pro-Gentile who is thrown out of the synagogue in his own town for reminding the congregation that the prophets had sometimes preferred Gentiles to Jews. In fact they try to throw him down from a sort of Tarpeian rock which they use for executions; but he makes his way through them and escapes: the only suggestion of a feat of arms on his part in the gospels. There is not a word of the Syrophœnician woman. At the end he is calmly superior to his sufferings; delivers an address on his way to execution with unruffled composure; does not despair on the cross; and dies with perfect dignity, commending his spirit to God, after praying for the forgiveness of his persecutors on the ground that 'They know not what they do'. According to Matthew, it is part of the bitterness of his death that even the thieves who are crucified with him revile him. According to Luke, only one of them does this; and he is rebuked by the other, who begs Jesus to remember him when he comes into his kingdom. To which Jesus replies, 'This day shalt thou be with me in Paradise', implying that he will spend the three days of his death there. In short, every device is used to get rid of the ruthless horror of the Matthew chronicle, and to relieve the strain of the Passion by touching episodes, and by representing Christ as superior to human suffering. It is Luke's Jesus who has won our hearts.

The Touch of Parisian Romance

Luke's romantic shrinking from unpleasantness, and his sentimentality, are illustrated by his version of the woman with the ointment. Matthew and Mark describe it as taking place in the house of Simon the Leper, where it is objected to as a waste of money. In Luke's version the leper becomes a rich Pharisee; the woman becomes a Dame aux Camellias;

and nothing is said about money and the poor. The woman washes the feet of Jesus with her tears and dries them with her hair; and he is reproached for suffering a sinful woman to touch him. It is almost an adaptation of the unromantic Matthew to the Parisian stage. There is a distinct attempt to increase the feminine interest all through. The slight lead given by Mark is taken up and developed. More is said about Jesus's mother and her feelings. Christ's following of women, just mentioned by Mark to account for their presence at his tomb, is introduced earlier; and some of the women are named; so that we are introduced to Joanna the wife of Chuza, Herod's steward, and Susanna. There is the quaint little domestic episode between Mary and Martha. There is the parable of the Prodigal Son, appealing to the indulgence romance has always shewn to Charles Surface and Des Grieux. Women follow Jesus to the cross; and he makes them a speech beginning 'Daughters of Jerusalem'. Slight as these changes may seem, they make a great change in the atmosphere. The Christ of Matthew could never have become what is vulgarly called a woman's hero (though the truth is that the popular demand for sentiment, as far as it is not simply human, is more manly than womanly); but the Christ of Luke has made possible those pictures which now hang in many ladies' chambers, in which Jesus is represented exactly as he is represented in the Lourdes cinematograph, by a handsome actor. The only touch of realism which Luke does not instinctively suppress for the sake of producing this kind of amenity is the reproach addressed to Jesus for sitting down to table without washing his hands; and that is retained because an interesting discourse hangs on it.

Waiting for the Messiah

Another new feature in Luke's story is that it begins in a world in which everyone is expecting the advent of the Christ. In Matthew and Mark, Jesus comes into a normal Philistine world like our own of today. Not until the Baptist foretells that one greater than himself shall come after him does the old Jewish hope of a Messiah begin to stir again; and as Jesus begins as a disciple of John, and is baptized by him, nobody connects him with that hope until Peter has the sudden inspiration which produces so startling an effect on Jesus. But in Luke's gospel men's minds, and especially women's minds, are full of eager expectation of a Christ not only before the birth of Jesus, but before the birth of John the Baptist, the event with which Luke begins his story. Whilst Jesus and John are still in their mothers' wombs, John leaps at the approach of Jesus when the two mothers visit one another. At the circumcision of Jesus pious men and women hail the infant as the Christ.

The Baptist himself is not convinced; for at quite a late period in his former disciple's career he sends two young men to ask Jesus is he really the Christ. This is noteworthy because Jesus immediately gives them a deliberate exhibition of miracles, and bids them tell John what they have seen, and ask him what he thinks *now*. This is in complete contradiction to what I have called the Rousseau view of miracles as inferred from Matthew. Luke shews all a romancer's thoughtlessness about miracles: he regards them as 'signs': that is, as proofs of the divinity of the person performing them, and not merely of thaumaturgic powers. He revels in miracles just as he revels in parables: they make such capital stories. He cannot allow the calling of Peter, James, and John from their boats to pass without a comic miraculous overdraft of fishes, with the net sinking the boats and

69

provoking Peter to exclaim, 'Depart from me; for I am a sinful man, O Lord,' which should probably be translated, 'I want no more of your miracles: natural fishing is good enough for my boats.'

There are some other novelties in Luke's version. Pilate sends Jesus to Herod, who happens to be in Jerusalem just then, because Herod had expressed some curiosity about him; but nothing comes of it: the prisoner will not speak to him. When Jesus is ill received in a Samaritan village James and John propose to call down fire from heaven and destroy it; and Jesus replies that he is come not to destroy lives but to save them. The bias of Jesus against lawyers is emphasized, and also his resolution not to admit that he is more bound to his relatives than to strangers. He snubs a woman who blesses his mother. As this is contrary to the traditions of sentimental romance, Luke would presumably have avoided it had he not become persuaded that the brotherhood of Man and the Fatherhood of God are superior even to sentimental considerations. The story of the lawyer asking what are the two chief commandments is changed by making Jesus put the question to the lawyer instead of answering it.

As to doctrine, Luke is only clear when his feelings are touched. His logic is weak; for some of the sayings of Jesus are pieced together wrongly, as anyone who has read them in the right order and context in Matthew will discover at once. He does not make anything new out of Christ's mission, and, like the other evangelists, thinks that the whole point of it is that Jesus was the long expected Christ, and that he will presently come back to earth and establish his kingdom, having duly died and risen again after three days. Yet Luke not only records the teaching as to communism and the discarding of hate, which have, of course, nothing to do with the Second Coming, but quotes one very remarkable saying which is not compatible with it, which is, that people must not go about asking where the kingdom of heaven is, and saying 'Lo, here!' and 'Lo, there!' because the kingdom of heaven is within them. But Luke has no sense that this belongs to a quite different order of thought to his Christianity, and retains undisturbed his view of the kingdom as a locality as definite as Jerusalem or Madagascar.

*   *   *

Credibility of the Gospels

It will be noted by the older among my readers, who are sure to be obsessed more or less by elderly wrangles as to whether the gospels are credible as matter-of-fact narratives, that I have hardly raised this question, and have accepted the credible and incredible with equal complacency. I have done this because credibility is a subjective condition, as the evolution of religious belief clearly shews. Belief is not dependent on evidence and reason. There is as much evidence that the miracles occurred as that the battle of Waterloo occurred, or that a large body of Russian troops passed through England in 1914 to take part in the war on the western front. The reasons for believing in the murder of Pompey are the same as the reasons for believing in the raising of Lazarus. Both have been believed and doubted by men of equal intelligence. Miracles, in the sense of phenomena we cannot explain, surround us on every hand: life itself is the miracle of miracles. Miracles in the sense of events that violate the normal course of our experience are vouched for every day: the flourishing Church of Christ Scientist is founded on a multitude of such miracles. Nobody believes all the miracles: everybody believes some of them. I cannot tell why men who will not believe that Jesus ever

71

existed yet believe firmly that Shakespear was Bacon. I cannot tell why people who believe that angels appeared and fought on our side at the battle of Mons, and who believe that miracles occur quite frequently at Lourdes, nevertheless boggle at the miracle of the liquefaction of the blood of St Januarius, and reject it as a trick of priestcraft. I cannot tell why people who will not believe Matthew's story of three kings bringing costly gifts to the cradle of Jesus, believe Luke's story of the shepherds and the stable. I cannot tell why people, brought up to believe the Bible in the old literal way as an infallible record and revelation, and rejecting that view later on, begin by rejecting the Old Testament, and give up the belief in a brimstone hell before they give up (if they ever do) the belief in a heaven of harps, crowns, and thrones. I cannot tell why people who will not believe in baptism on any terms believe in vaccination with the cruel fanaticism of inquisitors. I am convinced that if a dozen sceptics were to draw up in parallel columns a list of the events narrated in the gospels which they consider credible and incredible respectively, their lists would be different in several particulars. Belief is literally a matter of taste.

Fashions in Belief

Now matters of taste are mostly also matters of fashion. We are conscious of a difference between medieval fashions in belief and modern fashions. For instance, though we are more credulous than men were in the Middle Ages, and entertain such crowds of fortune-tellers, magicians, miracle workers, agents of communication with the dead, discoverers of the elixir of life, transmuters of metals, and healers of all sorts, as the Middle Ages never dreamed of as possible, yet we will not take our miracles in the form that convinced the

Middle Ages. Arithmetical numbers appealed to the Middle Ages just as they do to us, because they are difficult to deal with, and because the greatest masters of numbers, the Newtons and Leibnitzes, rank among the greatest men. But there are fashions in numbers too. The Middle Ages took a fancy to some familiar number like seven; and because it was an odd number, and the world was made in seven days, and there are seven stars in Charles's Wain, and for a dozen other reasons, they were ready to believe anything that had a seven or a seven times seven in it. Seven deadly sins, seven swords of sorrow in the heart of the Virgin, seven champions of Christendom, seemed obvious and reasonable things to believe in simply because they were seven. To us, on the contrary, the number seven is the stamp of superstition. We will believe in nothing less than millions. A medieval doctor gained his patient's confidence by telling him that his vitals were being devoured by seven worms. Such a diagnosis would ruin a modern physician. The modern physician tells his patient that he is ill because every drop of his blood is swarming with a million microbes; and the patient believes him abjectly and instantly. Had a bishop told William the Conqueror that the sun was seventy-seven miles distant from the earth, William would have believed him not only out of respect for the Church, but because he would have felt that seventy-seven miles was the proper distance. The Kaiser, knowing just as little about it as the Conqueror, would send that bishop to an asylum. Yet he (I presume) unhesitatingly accepts the estimate of ninety-two and nine-tenths millions of miles, or whatever the latest big figure may be.

Credibility and Truth

And here I must remind you that our credulity is not to be measured by the truth of the things we believe. When

men believed that the earth was flat, they were not credulous: they were using their common sense, and, if asked to
prove that the earth was flat, would have said simply, 'Look
at it.' Those who refuse to believe that it is round are exercis-
ing a wholesome scepticism. The modern man who believes
that the earth is round is grossly credulous. Flat Earth men
drive him to fury by confuting him with the greatest ease
when he tries to argue about it. Confront him with a theory
that the earth is cylindical, or annular, or hour-glass shaped,
and he is lost. The thing he believes may be true, but that is
not why he believes it: he believes it because in some
mysterious way it appeals to his imagination. If you ask him
why he believes that the sun is ninety-odd million miles off,
either he will have to confess that he doesn't know, or he
will say that Newton proved it. But he has not read the
treatise in which Newton proved it, and does not even know
that it was written in Latin. If you press an Ulster Protestant as to why he regards Newton as an infallible authority,
and St Thomas Aquinas or the Pope as superstitious liars
whom, after his death, he will have the pleasure of watching
from his place in heaven whilst they roast in eternal flame,
or if you ask me why I take into serious consideration
Colonel Sir Almroth Wright's estimates of the number of
streptococci contained in a given volume of serum whilst I
can only laugh at the earlier estimates of the number of
angels that can be accommodated on the point of a needle,
no reasonable reply is possible except that somehow sevens
and angels are out of fashion, and billions and streptococci
are all the rage. I simply cannot tell you why Bacon, Mon-
taigne, and Cervantes had a quite different fashion of
credulity and incredulity from the Venerable Bede and Piers
Plowman and the divine doctors of the Aquinas-Aristotle
school, who were certainly no stupider, and had the same
facts before them. Still less can I explain why, if we assume

74

that these leaders of thought had all reasoned out their beliefs, their authority seemed conclusive to one generation and blasphemous to another, neither generation having followed the reasoning or gone into the facts of the matter for itself at all.

It is therefore idle to begin disputing with the reader as to what he should believe in the gospels and what he should disbelieve. He will believe what he can, and disbelieve what he must. If he draws any lines at all, they will be quite arbitrary ones. St John tells us that when Jesus explicitly claimed divine honours by the sacrament of his body and blood, so many of his disciples left him that their number was reduced to twelve. Many modern readers will not hold out so long: they will give in at the first miracle. Others will discriminate. They will accept the healing miracles, and reject the feeding of the multitude. To some the walking on the water will be a legendary exaggeration of a swim, ending in an ordinary rescue of Peter; and the raising of Lazarus will be only a similar glorification of a commonplace feat of artificial respiration, whilst others will scoff at it as a planned imposture in which Lazarus acted as a confederate. Between the rejection of the stories as wholly fabulous and the acceptance of them as the evangelists themselves mean them to be accepted, there will be many shades of belief and disbelief, of sympathy and derision. It is not a question of being a Christian or not. A Mahometan Arab will accept literally and without question parts of the narrative which an English Archbishop has to reject or explain away; and many Theosophists and lovers of the wisdom of India, who never enter a Christian Church except as sightseers, will revel in parts of John's gospel which mean nothing to a pious matter-of-fact Bradford manufacturer. Every reader takes from the Bible what he can get. In submitting a précis of the gospel narratives I have not implied any estimate either

75

of their credibility or of their truth. I have simply informed him or reminded him, as the case may be, of what those narratives tell us about their hero.

Christian Iconolatry and the Peril of the Iconoclast

I must now abandon this attitude, and make a serious draft on the reader's attention by facing the question whether, if and when the medieval and Methodist will-to-believe the Salvationist and miraculous side of the gospel narratives fails us, as it plainly has failed the leaders of modern thought, there will be anything left of the mission of Jesus: whether, in short, we may not throw the gospels into the waste-paper basket, or put them away on the fiction shelf of our libraries. I venture to reply that we shall be, on the contrary, in the position of the man in Bunyan's riddle who found that 'the more he threw away, the more he had'. We get rid, to begin with, of the idolatrous or iconographic worship of Christ. By this I mean literally that worship which is given to pictures and statues of him, and to finished and unalterable stories about him. The test of the prevalence of this is that if you speak or write of Jesus as a real live person, or even as a still active God, such worshippers are more horrified than Don Juan was when the statue stepped from its pedestal and came to supper with him. You may deny the divinity of Jesus; you may doubt whether he ever existed; you may reject Christianity for Judaism, Mahometanism, Shintoism, or Fire Worship; and the iconolaters, placidly contemptuous, will only classify you as a freethinker or a heathen. But if you venture to wonder how Christ would have looked if he had shaved and had his hair cut, or what size in shoes he took, or whether he swore when he stood on a nail in the carpenter's shop, or could not

76

button his robe when he was in a hurry, or whether he laughed over the repartees by which he baffled the priests when they tried to trap him into sedition and blasphemy, or even if you tell any part of his story in the vivid terms of modern colloquial slang, you will produce an extraordinary dismay and horror among the iconolaters. You will have made the picture come out of its frame, the statue descend from its pedestal, the story become real, with all the incalculable consequences that may flow from this terrifying miracle. It is at such moments that you realize that the iconolaters have never for a moment conceived Christ as a real person who meant what he said, as a fact, as a force like electricity, only needing the invention of suitable political machinery to be applied to the affairs of mankind with revolutionary effect.

Thus it is not disbelief that is dangerous in our society: it is belief. The moment it strikes you (as it may any day) that Christ is not the lifeless harmless image he has hitherto been to you, but a rallying centre for revolutionary influences which all established States and Churches fight, you must look to yourselves; for you have brought the image to life; and the mob may not be able to bear that horror.

The Alternative to Barabbas

But mobs must be faced if civilization is to be saved. It did not need the present war to shew that neither the iconographic Christ nor the Christ of St Paul has succeeded in effecting the salvation of human society. Whilst I write, the Turks are said to be massacring the Armenian Christians on an unprecedented scale; but Europe is not in a position to remonstrate; for her Christians are slaying one another by every device which civilization has put within their reach as busily as they are slaying the Turks. Barabbas is triumphant everywhere; and the final use he makes of his triumph is to lead us all to suicide with heroic gestures and resounding lies. Now those who, like myself, see the Barabbasque social organization as a failure, and are convinced that the Life Force (or whatever you choose to call it) cannot be finally beaten by any failure, and will even supersede humanity by evolving a higher species if we cannot master the problems raised by the multiplication of our own numbers, have always known that Jesus has a real message, and have felt the fascination of his character and doctrine. Not that we should nowadays dream of claiming any supernatural authority for him, much less the technical authority which attaches to an educated modern philosopher and jurist. But when, having entirely got rid of Salvationist Christianity, and even contracted a prejudice against Jesus on the score of his involuntary connection with it, we engage on a purely scientific study of economics, criminology, and biology, and find that our practical conclusions are virtually those of Jesus, we are distinctly pleased and encouraged to find that we were doing him an injustice, and that the nimbus that surrounds his head in the pictures may be interpreted some day as a light of science rather than a declaration of sentiment or a label of idolatry.

The doctrines in which Jesus is thus confirmed are, roughly, the following:

1. The kingdom of heaven is within you. You are the son of God; and God is the son of man. God is a spirit, to be worshipped in spirit and in truth, and not an elderly gentleman to be bribed and begged from. We are members one of another; so that you cannot injure or help your neighbour without injuring or helping yourself. God is your father: you are here to do God's work; and you and your father are one.

2. Get rid of property by throwing it into the common stock. Dissociate your work entirely from money payments.

78

If you let a child starve you are letting God starve. Get rid of all anxiety about tomorrow's dinner and clothes, because you cannot serve two masters: God and Mammon.

3. Get rid of judges and punishment and revenge. Love your neighbour as yourself, he being a part of yourself. And love your enemies: they are your neighbours.

4. Get rid of your family entanglements. Every mother you meet is as much your mother as the woman who bore you. Every man you meet is as much your brother as the man she bore after you. Dont waste your time at family funerals grieving for your relatives: attend to life, not to death: there are as good fish in the sea as ever came out of it, and better. In the kingdom of heaven, which, as aforesaid, is within you, there is no marriage nor giving in marriage, because you cannot devote your life to two divinities: God and the person you are married to.

Now these are very interesting propositions; and they become more interesting every day, as experience and science drive us more and more to consider them favourably. In considering them, we shall waste our time unless we give them a reasonable construction. We must assume that the man who saw his way through such a mass of popular passion and illusion as stands between us and a sense of the value of such teaching was quite aware of all the objections that occur to an average stockbroker in the first five minutes. It is true that the world is governed to a considerable extent by the considerations that occur to stockbrokers in the first five minutes; but as the result is that the world is so badly governed that those who know the truth can hardly bear to live in it, an objection from an average stockbroker constitutes in itself a *prima facie* case for any social reform.

[1915]

Quot Homines, Tot Christi

The various images of Jesus that emerged from the fore-
going essay *On the Prospects of Christianity* set off a
series of letters to editors. Here, a year later, Shaw is still
talking back.

Originally the piece was an untitled response to comments in the *New Statesman*, and appeared on 17 June
1916. Shaw gave it the present heading when he was pre-
paring it for his collected works. The title is a variation of
Cicero's phrase, *Quot homines, tot causae*, 'As many men
as there are causes'. In Shaw's title: 'As many men as
there are Christs', or, perhaps, 'Every man his own Christ'.

I really must protest against the portraits of Jesus left to us
in the gospels being described as fancy portraits by me. It is
true that the three very distinct portraits by Matthew, Luke,
and John have long ago been combined into a composite
portrait, and overlaid by nearly 2,000 years of painting,
sculpture, legend, homily, theology, idealism, and sentimental fiction culminating in Miss Corelli's Barabbas and
Farrar's Life. So deeply have these repaintings affected our
consciousness of Jesus that it is almost impossible now to
read the gospels without reading into them all the mediaeval
conceptions, the Renaissance conceptions, the capitalistic
conceptions, and, in this country, the purely snobbish con-

ceptions which are as anachronistic in them as a telephone in the Garden of Eden. In the dry States of America, a teetotal conception is so insisted on that Churchmen write pamphlets to prove that the miracle of turning water into wine is founded on a Jacobean mistranslation of a Greek word which really means ginger beer.

I have done my best to disentangle the gospel biographies from their modern adulterations; and I am not surprised that Mr Desmond MacCarthy cannot express his contempt for the result. I was somewhat taken aback myself, though my emotion was not one of contempt. But it is useless to blame me for the shock. If I had chosen to write in the style of John Knox, I could have fortified with a text every sentence of the passage quoted by Mr MacCarthy. The ascetic Jesus, the virginal Jesus, the austerely moral Jesus, the beautifully dressed and scrupulously clean Jesus, the teetotal Jesus, like the snob Jesus of Anthony Trollope's parsons, is simply not in the gospels. He is absent not merely by default but by the express repudiation of Jesus himself, whose assertions of his kindly anti-ascetic view of life against that of John the Baptist I have sufficiently emphasized.

As to the notion that I have drawn Jesus in my own image, I do not see why Mr Desmond MacCarthy should deny us the fellowship of the Holy Ghost as the crown of our common humanity. Of course, Jesus was as like me as any one man is like another. Did Mr MacCarthy expect me to assume that one of us was a unicorn? I may go further, and claim that as we were both led to become preachers of the same doctrine in spite of different circumstances and by independent ways, I may reasonably be considered a little more like Jesus than, say – well, perhaps I had better name no names. At all events, whether Jesus be placed in a subspecies or in a super-species, it is a species to which I apparently belong philosophically.

81

But beyond this I cannot see that I have gone. I am not a faith healer. I am a teetotaller and vegetarian. I am reviled, not as a gluttonous man and a wine-bibber, but as what Mr Chesterton calls a Puritan. My appearances at rich men's feasts are so rare that my extra-domestic evening dress, though more than thirty years old, is still in excellent preservation. If any attempt is made to crucify me (and my dislike to blatant pseudo-patriotic nonsense may yet get me into trouble) I shall most certainly not submit as to a fatal ordeal and undertake to rise after three days. I could make out a better case for half a dozen of our public men as models for what Mr Cavendish Moxon calls 'my Jesus' (that in the critic's but a choleric word which in the author is flat blasphemy) than can be made out for me. Still, I shall not affect to regard the comparison as uncomplimentary. It is not in modest deprecation that I insist that 'my Jesus' is not mine at all, and not one and indivisible, but the three Jesuses of the gospels: the hard bigoted vituperative haughty Jesus of Matthew, the charming affable woman-beloved Jesus of Luke, and the restlessly intellectual debater, poet, and philosophic genius described by John. None of these may be the pet Jesus of the individual reader's idealizing vision; but I was not dealing with the various pet Jesuses any more than with the various pictured Christs of Van Eyck, of Durer, of Raphael, of Leonardo, of Michael Angelo, of Guido, of Rembrandt, of Rubens, of Noel Paton or Holman Hunt, of Burne-Jones, and of Von Uhde. All these are different; and the finest of them to my taste are repulsive to people who regard those which seem to me contemptible as official and authentic. In any case, it is clear that anyone writing about the historical Jesus must not write about Raphael's Transfiguration or Guido's Ecce Homo or Burne-Jones's figure in the east window of Speldhurst Church, but about the Christs of Matthew, Luke and

John and must face the fact that most readers will be astonished and scandalized at the restoration.

One correspondent is incredulous because 'Mr Shaw's Jesus' is not a damaged antique. He probably believes that Venus rose from the sea with her arms broken off; that Cœur de Lion lived in a picturesque ruin; and that Handel's harpsichord was worm-eaten and made a noise as of jangled bell wires. I will not attempt to disturb his belief in Progress.

Mr Desmond MacCarthy's simple and true observation that we cannot love ourselves is quite admirable; but I embrace its consequences. Am I to understand that Mr MacCarthy regards them as a *reductio ad absurdum*?

[1916]

The Infidel Half Century

In the 1890s Shaw mentioned in an off-hand manner his intention to write a 'gospel of Shawianity'. His Preface to *Back to Methuselah* comes closer than any other single work to fulfilling that intent.

The events of World War I, his genuine compassion for the suffering on both sides, and the storm of abuse heaped on him by patriots for his wartime sermons and scoldings produced, by 1920, a more sober and prophetic Shaw than the world had yet known. He was sixty-four and beginning to see himself as one of the elders, having no way of knowing how many years were left to him.

The full Preface – eighty-six pages in the Standard Edition – is a serious philosophical treatise. It is required reading for anyone who wants to ponder Shaw's mature thought. Even these excerpts, however, illustrate how demanding the need had become to formulate a religion that would give meaning to his political preachments – a creative evolution to vitalize his Fabian socialism.

The Dawn of Darwinism

One day early in the eighteen hundred and sixties, I, being then a small boy, was with my nurse, buying something in the shop of a petty newsagent, bookseller, and stationer in Camden Street, Dublin, when there entered an elderly man, weighty and solemn, who advanced to the counter, and said pompously, 'Have you the works of the celebrated Buffoon?'

My own works were at that time unwritten, or it is possible that the shop assistant might have misunderstood me so far as to produce a copy of Man and Superman. As it was, she knew quite well what he wanted; for this was before the Education Act of 1870 had produced shop assistants who know how to read and know nothing else. The celebrated Buffoon was not a humorist, but the famous naturalist Buffon. Every literate child at that time knew Buffon's Natural History as well as Esop's Fables. And no living child had heard the name that has since obliterated Buffon's in the popular consciousness: the name of Darwin.

Ten years elapsed. The celebrated Buffoon was forgotten; I had doubled my years and my length; and I had discarded the religion of my forefathers. One day the richest and consequently most dogmatic of my uncles came into a restaurant where I was dining, and found himself, much against his will, in conversation with the most questionable of his nephews. By way of making myself agreeable, I spoke of modern thought and Darwin. He said, 'Oh, thats the fellow who wants to make out that we all have tails like monkeys.' I tried to explain that what Darwin had insisted on in this connection was that some monkeys have no tails. But my uncle was as impervious to what Darwin really said as any Neo-Darwinian nowadays. He died impenitent, and did not mention me in his will.

Twenty years elapsed. If my uncle had been alive, he would have known all about Darwin, and known it all wrong. In spite of the efforts of Grant Allen to set him right, he would have accepted Darwin as the discoverer of Evolution, of Heredity, and of modification of species by Selection. For the pre-Darwinian age had come to be regarded as a Dark Age in which men still believed that the book of

Genesis was a standard scientific treatise, and that the only additions to it were Galileo's demonstration of Leonardo da Vinci's simple remark that the earth is a moon of the sun, Newton's theory of gravitation, Sir Humphry Davy's invention of the safety-lamp, the discovery of electricity, the application of steam to industrial purposes, and the penny post. It was just the same in other subjects. Thus Nietzsche, by the two or three who had come across his writings, was supposed to have been the first man to whom it occurred that mere morality and legality and urbanity lead nowhere, as if Bunyan had never written Badman. Schopenhauer was credited with inventing the distinction between the Covenant of Grace and the Covenant of Works which troubled Cromwell on his deathbed. People talked as if there had been no dramatic or descriptive music before Wagner; no impressionist painting before Whistler; whilst as to myself, I was finding that the surest way to produce an effect of daring innovation and originality was to revive the ancient attraction of long rhetorical speeches; to stick closely to the methods of Molière; and to lift characters bodily out of the pages of Charles Dickens.

The Advent of the Neo-Darwinians

This particular sort of ignorance does not always or often matter. But in Darwin's case it did matter. If Darwin had really led the world at one bound from the book of Genesis to Heredity, to Modification of Species by Selection, and to Evolution, he would have been a philosopher and a prophet as well as an eminent professional naturalist, with geology as a hobby. The delusion that he had actually achieved this feat did no harm at first, because if people's views are sound, about evolution or anything else, it does not make two straws difference whether they call the revealer of their views Tom or Dick. But later on such apparently negligible errors have awkward consequences. Darwin was given an imposing reputation as not only an Evolutionist, but as *the* Evolutionist, with the immense majority who never read his books. The few who never read any others were led by them to concentrate exclusively on Circumstantial Selection as the explanation of all the transformations and adaptations which were the evidence for Evolution. And they presently found themselves so cut off by this specialization from the majority who knew Darwin only by his spurious reputation, that they were obliged to distinguish themselves, not as Darwinians, but as Neo-Darwinians.

Before ten more years had elapsed, the Neo-Darwinians were practically running current Science. It was 1906; I was fifty; I published my own view of evolution in a play called Man and Superman; and I found that most people were unable to understand how I could be an Evolutionist and not a Neo-Darwinian, or why I habitually derided Neo-Darwinism as a ghastly idiocy, and would fall on its professors slaughterously in public discussions. It was in the hope of making me clear the matter up that the Fabian Society, which was then organizing a series of lectures on Prophets of the Nineteenth Century, asked me to deliver a lecture on the prophet Darwin. I did so; and scraps of that lecture, which was never published, variegate these pages.

Political Inadequacy of the Human Animal

Ten more years elapsed. Neo-Darwinism in politics had produced a European catastrophe of a magnitude so appalling, and a scope so unpredictable, that as I write these lines in 1920, it is still far from certain whether our civilization will survive it. The circumstances of this catastrophe, the boyish cinema-fed romanticism which made it possible to impose it on the people as a crusade, and especially the ignorance and errors of the victors of Western Europe when its violent phase had passed and the time for reconstruction arrived, confirmed a doubt which had grown steadily in my mind during my forty years public work as a Socialist: namely, whether the human animal, as he exists at present, is capable of solving the social problems raised by his own aggregation, or, as he calls it, his civilization.

Cowardice of the Irreligious

Another observation I had made was that goodnatured unambitious men are cowards when they have no religion. They are dominated and exploited not only by greedy and often half-witted and half-alive weaklings who will do anything for cigars, champagne, motor cars, and the more childish and selfish uses of money, but by able and sound administrators who can do nothing else with them than dominate and exploit them. Government and exploitation become synonymous under such circumstances; and the world is finally ruled by the childish, the brigands, and the blackguards. Those who refuse to stand in with them are persecuted and occasionally executed when they give any trouble to the exploiters. They fall into poverty when they lack lucrative specific talents. At the present moment one half of Europe, having knocked the other half down, is trying to kick it to death, and may succeed: a procedure which is, logically, sound Neo-Darwinism. And the goodnatured majority are looking on in helpless horror, or allowing themselves to be persuaded by the newspapers of their exploiters that the kicking is not only a sound commercial investment, but an act of divine justice of which they are the ardent instruments.

Flimsiness of Civilization

This situation has occurred so often before, always with the same result of a collapse of civilization (Professor Flinders Petrie has let out the secret of previous collapses), that the rich are instinctively crying 'Let us eat and drink; for tomorrow we die', and the poor, 'How long, O Lord, how long?' But the pitiless reply still is that God helps those who help themselves. This does not mean that if Man cannot find the remedy no remedy will be found. The power that produced Man when the monkey was not up to the mark, can produce a higher creature than Man if Man does not come up to the mark. What it means is that if Man is to be saved, Man must save himself. There seems no compelling reason why he should be saved. He is by no means an ideal creature. At his present best many of his ways are so unpleasant that they are unmentionable in polite society, and so painful that he is compelled to pretend that pain is often a good. Nature holds no brief for the human experiment: it must stand or fall by its results. If Man will not serve, Nature will try another experiment.

What hope is there then of human improvement? According to the Neo-Darwinists, to the Mechanists, no hope whatever, because improvement can come only through some senseless accident which must, on the statistical average of accidents, be presently wiped out by some other equally senseless accident.

Creative Evolution

But this dismal creed does not discourage those who believe that the impulse that produces evolution is creative. They have observed the simple fact that the will to do anything can and does, at a certain pitch of intensity set up by conviction of its necessity, create and organize new tissue to do

89

it with. To them therefore mankind is by no means played out yet. If the weight lifter, under the trivial stimulus of an athletic competition, can 'put up a muscle', it seems reasonable to believe that an equally earnest and convinced philosopher could 'put up a brain'. Both are directions of vitality to a certain end. Evolution shews us this direction of vitality doing all sorts of things: providing the centipede with a hundred legs, and ridding the fish of any legs at all; building lungs and arms for the land and gills and fins for the sea; enabling the mammal to gestate its young inside its body, and the fowl to incubate hers outside it; offering us, we may say, our choice of any sort of bodily contrivance to maintain our activity and increase our resources.

Voluntary Longevity

Among other matters apparently changeable at will is the duration of individual life. Weismann, a very clever and suggestive biologist who was unhappily reduced to idiocy by Neo-Darwinism, pointed out that death is not an eternal condition of life, but an expedient introduced to provide for continual renewal without overcrowding. Now Circumstantial Selection does not account for natural death: it accounts only for the survival of species in which the individuals have sense enough to decay and die on purpose. But the individuals do not seem to have calculated very reasonably: nobody can explain why a parrot should live ten times as long as a dog, and a turtle be almost immortal. In the case of man, the operation has overshot its mark: men do not live long enough: they are, for all the purposes of high civilization, mere children when they die; and our Prime Ministers, though rated as mature, divide their time between the golf course and the Treasury Bench in parliament. Presumably, however, the same power that made this mistake can remedy it. If on opportunist grounds Man now fixes the term of his life at three score and ten years, he can equally fix it at three hundred, or three thousand, or even at the genuine Circumstantial Selection limit, which would be until a sooner-or-later-inevitable fatal accident makes an end of the individual. All that is necessary to make him extend his present span is that tremendous catastrophes such as the late war shall convince him of the necessity of at least outliving his taste for golf and cigars if the race is to be saved. This is not fantastic speculation: it is deductive biology, if there is such a science as biology. Here, then, is a stone that we have left unturned, and that may be worth turning. To make the suggestion more entertaining than it would be to most people in the form of a biological treatise, I have written Back to Methuselah as a contribution to the modern Bible.

*   *   *

The Advent of the Neo-Lamarckians

I call your special attention to Lamarck, because later on there were Neo-Lamarckians as well as Neo-Darwinians. I was a Neo-Lamarckian. Lamarck passed on from the conception of Evolution as a general law to Charles Darwin's department of it, which was the method of Evolution. Lamarck, whilst making many ingenious suggestions as to the reaction of external causes on life and habit, such as changes of climate, food supply, geological upheavals and so forth, really held as his fundamental proposition that living organisms changed because they wanted to. As he stated it, the great factor in Evolution is use and disuse. If you have no eyes, and want to see, and keep trying to see, you will finally get eyes. If, like a mole or a subterranean fish, you have eyes and dont want to see, you will lose your eyes. If you like eating the tender tops of trees enough to

91

make you concentrate all your energies on the stretching of your neck, you will finally get a long neck, like the giraffe. This seems absurd to inconsiderate people at the first blush; but it is within the personal experience of all of us that it is just by this process that a child tumbling about the floor becomes a boy walking erect; and that a man sprawling on the road with a bruised chin, or supine on the ice with a bashed occiput, becomes a bicyclist and a skater. The process is not continuous, as it would be if mere practice had anything to do with it; for though you may improve at each bicycling lesson *during* the lesson, when you begin your next lesson you do not begin at the point at which you left off: you relapse apparently to the beginning. Finally, you succeed quite suddenly, and do not relapse again. More miraculous still, you at once exercise the new power unconsciously. Although you are adapting your front wheel to your balance so elaborately and actively that the accidental locking of your handlebars for a second will throw you off; though five minutes before you could not do it at all, yet now you do it as unconsciously as you grow your finger nails. You have a new faculty, and must have created some new bodily tissue as its organ. And you have done it solely by willing. For here there can be no question of Circumstantial Selection, or the survival of the fittest. The man who is learning how to ride a bicycle has no advantage over the non-cyclist in the struggle for existence: quite the contrary. He has acquired a new habit, an automatic unconscious habit, solely because he wanted to, and kept trying until it was added unto him.

How Acquirements are Inherited

But when your son tries to skate or bicycle in his turn, he does not pick up the accomplishment where you left it, any more than he is born six feet high with a beard and a tall hat. The set-back that occurred between your lessons occurs again. The race learns exactly as the individual learns. Your son relapses, not to the very beginning, but to a point which no mortal method of measurement can distinguish from the beginning. Now this is odd; for certain other habits of yours, equally acquired (to the Evolutionist, of course, all habits are acquired), equally unconscious, equally automatic, are transmitted without any perceptible relapse. For instance, the very first act of your son when he enters the world as a separate individual is to yell with indignation: that yell which Shakespear thought the most tragic and piteous of all sounds. In the act of yelling he begins to breathe: another habit, and not even a necessary one, as the object of breathing can be achieved in other ways, as by deep sea fishes. He circulates his blood by pumping it with his heart. He demands a meal, and proceeds at once to perform the most elaborate chemical operations on the food he swallows. He manufactures teeth; discards them; and replaces them with fresh ones. Compared to these habitual feats, walking, standing upright, and bicycling are the merest trifles; yet it is only by going through the wanting, trying process that he can stand, walk, or cycle, whereas in the other and far more difficult and complex habits he not only does not consciously want nor consciously try, but actually consciously objects very strongly. Take that early habit of cutting the teeth: would he do that if he could help it? Take that later habit of decaying and eliminating himself by death — equally an acquired habit, remember — how he abhors it! Yet the habit has become so rooted, so automatic, that he must do it in spite of himself, even to his own destruction.

We have here a routine which, given time enough for it to operate, will finally produce the most elaborate forms of organized life on Lamarckian lines without the intervention of Circumstantial Selection at all. If you can turn a pedestrian into a cyclist, and a cyclist into a pianist or violinist, without the intervention of Circumstantial Selection, you can turn an amoeba into a man, or a man into a superman, without it. All of which is rank heresy to the Neo-Darwinian, who imagines that if you stop Circumstantial Selection, you not only stop development but inaugurate a rapid and disastrous degeneration.

Let us fix the Lamarckian evolutionary process well in our minds. You are alive; and you want to be more alive. You want an extension of consciousness and of power. You want, consequently, additional organs, or additional uses of your existing organs: that is, additional habits. You get them because you want them badly enough to keep trying for them until they come. Nobody knows how: nobody knows why: all we know is that the thing actually takes place. We relapse miserably from effort to effort until the old organ is modified or the new one created, when suddenly the impossible becomes possible and the habit is formed. The moment we form it we want to get rid of the consciousness of it so as to economize our consciousness for fresh conquests of life; as all consciousness means preoccupation and obstruction. If we had to think about breathing or digesting or circulating our blood we should have no attention to spare for anything else, as we find to our cost when anything goes wrong with these operations. We want to be unconscious of them just as we wanted to acquire them; and we finally win what we want. But we win unconsciousness of our habits at the cost of losing our control of them; and we also build one habit and its corresponding functional modification of our organs on another, and so become dependent on our old habits. Consequently we have to persist in them even when they hurt us. We cannot stop breathing to avoid an attack of asthma, or to escape drowning. We can lose a habit and discard an organ when we no longer need them, just as we acquired them; but this process is slow and broken by relapses; and relics of the organ and the habit long survive its utility. And if other and still indispensable habits and modifications have been built on the ones we wish to discard, we must provide a new foundation for them before we demolish the old one. This is also a slow process and a very curious one.

*   *   *

Heredity an Old Story

It is evident that the evolutionary process is a hereditary one, or, to put it less drily, that human life is continuous and immortal. The Evolutionists took heredity for granted. So did everybody. The human mind has been soaked in heredity as long back as we can trace its thought. Hereditary peers, hereditary monarchs, hereditary castes and trades and classes were the best known of social institutions, and in some cases of public nuisances. Pedigree men counted pedigree dogs and pedigree horses among their most cherished possessions. Far from being unconscious of heredity, or sceptical, men were insanely credulous about it: they not only believed in the transmission of qualities and habits from generation to generation, but expected the son to begin mentally where the father left off.

This belief in heredity led naturally to the practice of Intentional Selection. Good blood and breeding were eagerly sought after in human marriage. In dealing with plants and animals, selection with a view to the production of new varieties and the improvement and modification of species had been practised ever since men began to cultivate them. My pre-Darwinian uncle knew as well as Darwin that the race-horse and the dray-horse are not separate creations from the Garden of Eden, but adaptations by deliberate human selection of the medieval war-horse to modern racing and industrial haulage. He knew that there are nearly two hundred different sorts of dogs, all capable of breeding with one another and of producing cross varieties unknown to Adam. He knew that the same thing is true of pigeons. He knew that gardeners had spent their lives trying to breed black tulips and green carnations and unheard-of orchids, and had actually produced flowers just as strange to Eve. His quarrel with the Evolutionists was not a quarrel with the evidence for Evolution: he had accepted enough of it to prove Evolution ten times over before he ever heard of it. What he repudiated was cousinship with the ape, and the implied suspicion of a rudimentary tail, because it was offensive to his sense of his own dignity, and because he thought that apes were ridiculous, and tails diabolical when associated with the erect posture. Also he believed that Evolution was a heresy which involved the destruction of Christianity, of which, as a member of the Irish Church (the pseudo-Protestant one), he conceived himself a pillar. But this was only his ignorance; for man may deny his descent from an ape and be eligible as a churchwarden without being any the less a convinced Evolutionist.

* * *

Defying the lightning: a frustrated experiment

One evening in 1878 or thereabouts, I, being then in my earliest twenties, was at a bachelor party of young men of the professional class in the house of a doctor in the Kensingtonian quarter of London. They fell to talking about religious revivals; and an anecdote was related of a man who, having incautiously scoffed at the mission of Messrs

Moody and Sankey, a then famous firm of American evangelists, was subsequently carried home on a shutter, slain by divine vengeance as a blasphemer. A timid minority, without quite venturing to question the truth of the incident – for they naturally did not care to run the risk of going home on shutters themselves – nevertheless shewed a certain disposition to cavil at those who exulted in it; and something approaching to an argument began. At last it was alleged by the most evangelical of the disputants that Charles Bradlaugh, the most formidable atheist on the Secularist platform, had taken out his watch publicly and challenged the Almighty to strike him dead in five minutes if he really existed and disapproved of atheism. The leader of the cavillers, with great heat, repudiated this as a gross calumny, declaring that Bradlaugh had repeatedly and indignantly contradicted it, and implying that the atheist champion was far too pious a man to commit such a blasphemy. This exquisite confusion of ideas roused my sense of comedy. It was clear to me that the challenge attributed to Charles Bradlaugh was a scientific experiment of a quite simple, straightforward, and proper kind to ascertain whether the expression of atheistic opinions really did involve any personal risk. It was certainly the method taught in the Bible, Elijah having confuted the prophets of Baal in precisely that way, with every circumstance of bitter mockery of their god when he failed to send down fire from heaven. Accordingly I said that if the question at issue were whether the penalty of questioning the theology of Messrs Moody and Sankey was to be struck dead on the spot by an incensed deity, nothing could effect a more convincing settlement of it than the very obvious experiment attributed to Mr Bradlaugh, and that consequently if he had not tried it, he ought to have tried it. The omission, I added, was one which could easily be remedied there and then, as I

97

happened to share Mr Bradlaugh's views as to the absurdity of the belief in these violent interferences with the order of nature by a short-tempered and thin-skinned supernatural deity. Therefore – and at that point I took out my watch.

The effect was electrical. Neither sceptics nor devotees were prepared to abide the result of the experiment. In vain did I urge the pious to trust in the accuracy of their deity's aim with a thunderbolt, and the justice of his discrimination between the innocent and the guilty. In vain did I appeal to the sceptics to accept the logical outcome of their scepticism: it soon appeared that when thunderbolts were in question there were no sceptics. Our host, seeing that his guests would vanish precipitately if the impious challenge were uttered, leaving him alone with a solitary infidel under sentence of extermination in five minutes, interposed and forbade the experiment, pleading at the same time for a change of subject. I of course complied, but could not refrain from remarking that though the dreadful words had not been uttered, yet, as the thought had been formulated in my mind it was very doubtful whether the consequences could be averted by sealing my lips. However, the rest appeared to feel that the game would be played according to the rules, and that it mattered very little what I thought so long as I said nothing. Only the leader of the evangelical party, I thought, was a little preoccupied until five minutes had elapsed and the weather was still calm.

* * *

Paley's Watch

Paley had put the argument in an apparently unanswerable form. If you found a watch, full of mechanism exquisitely adapted to produce a series of operations all leading to the fulfilment of one central purpose of measuring for mankind the march of the day and night, could you believe that it was not the work of a cunning artificer who had designed and contrived it all to that end? And here was a far more wonderful thing than a watch, a man with all his organs ingeniously contrived, cords and levers, girders and king-posts, circulating systems of pipes and valves, dialysing membranes, chemical retorts, carburettors, ventilators, inlets and outlets, telephone transmitters in his ears, light recorders and lenses in his eye: was it conceivable that this was the work of chance? that no artificer had wrought here? that there was no purpose in this, no design, no guiding intelligence? The thing was incredible.

*   *   *

The Moment and the Man

This superstition of a continual capricious disorder in nature, of a lawgiver who was also a lawbreaker, made atheists in all directions among clever and lightminded people. But atheism did not account for Paley's watch. Atheism accounted for nothing; and it was the business of science to account for everything that was plainly accountable. Science had no use for mere negation: what was desired by it above all things just then was a demonstration that the evidences of design could be explained without resort to the hypothesis of a personal designer. If only some genius, whilst admitting Paley's facts, could knock the brains out of Paley by the discovery of a method whereby watches could happen without watchmakers, that genius was assured of such a welcome from the thought of his day as no natural philosopher had ever enjoyed before.

The time being thus ripe, the genius appeared; and his

name was Charles Darwin. And now, what did Darwin really discover?

Here, I am afraid, I shall require once more the assistance of the giraffe, or, as he was called in the days of the celebrated Buffoon, the camelopard (by children, cammy-leopard). I do not remember how this animal imposed himself illustratively on the Evolution controversy; but there was no getting away from him then; and I am old-fashioned enough to be unable to get away from him now. How did he come by his long neck? Lamarck would have said, by wanting to get at the tender leaves high up on the tree, and trying until he succeeded in wishing the necessary length of neck into existence. Another answer was also possible: namely, that some prehistoric stockbreeder, wishing to produce a natural curiosity, selected the longest-necked animals he could find, and bred from them until at last an animal with an abnormally long neck was evolved by intentional selection, just as the race-horse or the fantail pigeon has been evolved. Both these explanations, you will observe, involve consciousness, will, design, purpose, either on the part of the animal itself or on the part of a superior intelligence controlling its destiny. Darwin pointed out – and this and no more was Darwin's famous discovery – that a third explanation, involving neither will nor purpose nor design either in the animal or anyone else, was on the cards. If your neck is too short to reach your food, you die. That may be the simple explanation of the fact that all the surviving animals that feed on foliage have necks or trunks long enough to reach it. So bang goes your belief that the necks must have been designed to reach the food. But Lamarck did not believe that the necks were so designed in the beginning: he believed that the long necks were evolved by wanting and trying. Not necessarily, said Darwin. Consider the effect on the giraffes of the natural multiplication of their numbers, as insisted on by Malthus. Suppose the average height of the foliage-eating animals is four feet, and that they increase in numbers until a time comes when all the trees are eaten away to within four feet of the ground. Then the animals who happen to be an inch or two short of the average will die of starvation. All the animals who happen to be an inch or so above the average will be better fed and stronger than the others. They will secure the strongest and tallest mates; and their progeny will survive whilst the average ones and the sub-average ones will die out. This process, by which the species gains, say, an inch in reach, will repeat itself until the giraffe's neck is so long that he can always find food enough within his reach, at which point, of course, the selective process stops and the length of the giraffe's neck stops with it. Otherwise, he would grow until he could browse off the trees in the moon. And this, mark you, without the intervention of any stockbreeder, human or divine, and without will, purpose, design, or even consciousness beyond the blind will to satisfy hunger. It is true that this blind will, being in effect a will to live, gives away the whole case; but still, as compared to the open-eyed intelligent wanting and trying of Lamarck, the Darwinian process may be described as a chapter of accidents. As such, it seems simple, because you do not at first realize all that it involves. But when its whole significance dawns on you, your heart sinks into a heap of sand within you. There is a hideous fatalism about it, a ghastly and damnable reduction of beauty and intelligence, of strength and purpose, of honour and aspiration, to such casually picturesque changes as an avalanche may make in a mountain landscape, or a railway accident in a human figure. To call this Natural Selection is a blasphemy, possible to many for whom Nature is nothing but a casual aggregation of inert and dead matter, but eternally impossible to the spirits and souls of the righteous. If it be no blasphemy, but a truth of science, then the stars of heaven, the showers and dew, the winter and summer, the fire and heat, the mountains and hills, may no longer be called to exalt the Lord with us by praise; their work is to modify all things by blindly starving and murdering everything that is not lucky enough to survive in the universal struggle for hogwash.

The Brink of the Bottomless Pit

Thus did the neck of the giraffe reach out across the whole heavens and make men believe that what they saw there was a gloaming of the gods. For if this sort of selection could turn an antelope into a giraffe, it could conceivably turn a pond full of amoebas into the French Academy. Though Lamarck's way, the way of life, will, aspiration, and achievement, remained still possible, this newly shewn way of hunger, death, stupidity, delusion, chance, and bare survival was also possible: was indeed most certainly the way in which many apparently intelligently designed transformations had actually come to pass. . . . When Napoleon was asked what would happen when he died, he said that Europe would express its intense relief with a great 'Ouf!': Well, when Darwin killed the god who objected to chloroform, everybody who had ever thought about it said 'Ouf!' Paley was buried fathoms deep with his watch, now fully accounted for without any divine artificer at all. We were so glad to be rid of both that we never gave a thought to the consequences. . . . If I had told that uncle of mine that within thirty years from the date of our conversation I should be exposing myself to suspicions of the grossest superstition by questioning the sufficiency of Darwin; maintaining the reality of the Holy Ghost; declaring that the phenomenon of the Word becoming Flesh was occurring daily, he would have regarded me as the most extravagant madman our family had ever produced. Yet it was so. In 1906 I might have vituperated Jehovah more heartily than ever Shelley did without eliciting a protest in any circle of thinkers, or shocking any public audience accustomed to modern discussion; but when I described Darwin as 'an intelligent and industrious pigeon fancier', that blasphemous levity, as it seemed, was received with horror and indignation. The tide has now turned; and every puny whipster may say what he likes about Darwin; but anyone who wants to know what it was to be a Lamarckian during the last quarter of the nineteenth century has only to read Mr Festing Jones's memoir of Samuel Butler to learn how completely even a man of genius could isolate himself by antagonizing Darwin on the one hand and the Church on the other.

Why Darwin Converted the Crowd

I am well aware that in describing the effect of Darwin's discovery on naturalists and on persons capable of serious reflection on the nature and attributes of God, I am leaving the vast mass of the British public out of account. I have pointed out elsewhere that the British nation does not consist of atheists and Plymouth Brothers; and I am not now going to pretend that it ever consisted of Darwinians and Lamarckians. The average citizen is irreligious and unscientific: you talk to him about cricket and golf, market prices and party politics, not about evolution and relativity, transubstantiation and predestination. Nothing will knock into his head the fateful distinction between Evolution as promulgated by Erasmus Darwin, and Circumstantial (so-called Natural) Selection as revealed by his grandson. Yet the doctrine of Charles reached him, though the doctrine of

Erasmus had passed over his head. Why did not Erasmus Darwin popularize the word Evolution as effectively as Charles?

The reason was, I think, that Circumstantial Selection is easier to understand, more visible and concrete, than Lamarckian evolution. Evolution as a philosophy and physiology of the will is a mystical process, which can be apprehended only by a trained, apt, and comprehensive thinker. Though the phenomena of use and disuse, of wanting and trying, of the manufacture of weight lifters and wrestlers from men of ordinary strength, are familiar enough as facts, they are extremely puzzling as subjects of thought, and lead you into metaphysics the moment you try to account for them. But pigeon fanciers, dog fanciers, gardeners, stock breeders, or stud grooms, can understand Circumstantial Selection, because it is their business to produce transformation by imposing on flowers and animals a Selection From Without. All that Darwin had to say to them was that the mere chapter of accidents is always doing on a huge scale what they themselves are doing on a very small scale. There is hardly a labourer attached to an English country house who has not taken a litter of kittens or puppies to the bucket, and drowned all of them except the one he thinks the most promising. Such a man has nothing to learn about the survival of the fittest except that it acts in more ways than he has yet noticed; for he knows quite well, as you will find if you are not too proud to talk to him, that this sort of selection occurs naturally (in Darwin's sense) too: that, for instance, a hard winter will kill off a weakly child as the bucket kills off a weakly puppy. Then there is the farm labourer. Shakespear's Touchstone, a court-bred fool, was shocked to find in the shepherd a natural philosopher, and opined that he would be damned for the part he took in the sexual selection of sheep. As to the production of new species by the selection of variations, that is no news to your gardener. Now if you are familiar with these three processes: the survival of the fittest, sexual selection, and variation leading to new kinds, there is nothing to puzzle you in Darwinism.

That was the secret of Darwin's popularity. He never puzzled anybody. If very few of us have read The Origin of Species from end to end, it is not because it overtaxes our mind, but because we take in the whole case and are prepared to accept it long before we have come to the end of the innumerable instances and illustrations of which the book mainly consists. Darwin becomes tedious in the manner of a man who insists on continuing to prove his innocence after he has been acquitted. You assure him that there is not a stain on his character, and beg him to leave the court; but he will not be content with enough evidence: he will have you listen to all the evidence that exists in the world. Darwin's industry was enormous. His patience, his perseverance, his conscientiousness reached the human limit. But he never got deeper beneath or higher above his facts than an ordinary man could follow him. He was not conscious of having raised a stupendous issue, because, though it arose instantly, it was not his business. He was conscious of having discovered a process of transformation and modification which accounted for a great deal of natural history. But he did not put it forward as accounting for the whole of natural history. . . . In short, he was not a Darwinian, but an honest naturalist working away at his job with so little preoccupation with theological speculation that he never quarrelled with the theistic Unitarianism into which he was born, and remained to the end the engagingly simple and socially easy-going soul he had been in his boyhood, when his elders doubted whether he would ever be of much use in the world.

How we Rushed Down a Steep Place

Not so the rest of us intellectuals. We all began going to the devil with the utmost cheerfulness. Everyone who had a mind to change, changed it. Only Samuel Butler, on whom Darwin had acted homeopathically, reacted against him furiously; ran up the Lamarckian flag to the top-gallant peak; declared with penetrating accuracy that Darwin had 'banished mind from the universe'; and even attacked Darwin's personal character, unable to bear the fact that the author of so abhorrent a doctrine was an amiable and upright man.... We were intellectually intoxicated with the idea that the world could make itself without design, purpose, skill, or intelligence: in short, without life.

*   *   *

Ever since [Darwin] set up Circumstantial Selection as the creator and ruler of the universe, the scientific world has been the very citadel of stupidity and cruelty. Fearful as the tribal god of the Hebrews was, nobody ever shuddered as they passed even his meanest and narrowest Little Bethel or his proudest war-consecrating cathedral as we shudder now when we pass a physiological laboratory. If we dreaded and mistrusted the priest, we could at least keep him out of the house; but what of the modern Darwinist surgeon whom we dread and mistrust ten times more, but into whose hands we must all give ourselves from time to time? Miserably as religion had been debased, it did at least still proclaim that our relation to one another was that of a fellowship in which we were all equal and members one of another before the judgment-seat of our common father. Darwinism proclaimed that our true relation is that of competitors and combatants in a struggle for mere survival, and that every act of pity or loyalty to the old fellowship is a vain and mischievous attempt to lessen the severity of the struggle and preserve inferior varieties from the efforts of Nature to weed them out. Even in Socialist Societies which existed solely to substitute the law of fellowship for the law of competition, and the method of providence and wisdom for the method of rushing violently down a steep place into the sea, I found myself regarded as a blasphemer and an ignorant sentimentalist because whenever the Neo-Darwinian doctrine was preached there I made no attempt to conceal my intellectual contempt for its blind coarseness and shallow logic, or my natural abhorrence of its sickening inhumanity.

The Greatest of these is Self-control

As there is no place in Darwinism for free will, or any other sort of will, the Neo-Darwinists held that there is no such thing as self-control. Yet self-control is just the one quality of survival value which Circumstantial Selection must invariably and inevitably develop in the long run. Uncontrolled qualities may be selected for survival and development for certain periods and under certain circumstances. For instance, since it is the ungovernable gluttons who strive the hardest to get food and drink, their efforts would develop their strength and cunning in a period of such scarcity that the utmost they could do would not enable them to over-eat themselves. But a change of circumstances involving a plentiful supply of food would destroy them. We see this very thing happening often enough in the case of the healthy and vigorous poor man who becomes a millionaire by one of the accidents of our competitive commerce, and immediately proceeds to dig his grave with his teeth. But the self-controlled man survives all such changes of circumstance, because he adapts himself to them, and eats neither as much as he can hold nor as little as he can scrape along on, but as much as is good for him. What *is* self-control? It is nothing but a highly developed vital sense, dominating and regulating the mere appetites. To overlook the very existence of this supreme sense; to miss the obvious inference that it is the quality that distinguishes the fittest to survive; to omit, in short, the highest moral claim of Evolutionary Selection: all this, which the Neo-Darwinians did in the name of Natural Selection, shewed the most pitiable want of mastery of their own subject, the dullest lack of observation of the forces upon which Natural Selection works.

*　　*　　*

The Humanitarians and the Problem of Evil

Yet the humanitarians were as delighted as anybody with Darwinism at first. They had been perplexed by the Problem of Evil and the Cruelty of Nature. They were Shelley-ists, but not atheists. Those who believed in God were at a terrible disadvantage with the atheist. They could not deny the existence of natural facts so cruel that to attribute them to the will of God is to make God a demon. Belief in God was impossible to any thoughtful person without belief in the Devil as well. The painted Devil, with his horns, his barbed tail, and his abode of burning brimstone, was an incredible bogey; but the evil attributed to him was real enough; and the atheists argued that the author of evil, if he exists, must be strong enough to overcome God, else God is morally responsible for everything he permits the Devil to do. Neither conclusion delivered us from the horror of attributing the cruelty of nature to the workings of an evil will, or could reconcile it with our impulses towards justice, mercy, and a higher life.

A complete deliverance was offered by the discovery of

Circumstantial Selection: that is to say, of a method by which horrors having every appearance of being elaborately planned by some intelligent contriver are only accidents without any moral significance at all. Suppose a watcher from the stars saw a frightful accident produced by two crowded trains at full speed crashing into one another! How could he conceive that a catastrophe brought about by such elaborate machinery, such ingenious preparation, such skilled direction, such vigilant industry, was quite unintentional? Would he not conclude that the signal-men were devils?

Well, Circumstantial Selection is largely a theory of collisions: that is, a theory of the innocence of much apparently designed devilry. In this way Darwin brought intense relief as well as an enlarged knowledge of facts to the humanitarians. He destroyed the omnipotence of God for them; but he also exonerated God from a hideous charge of cruelty. Granted that the comfort was shallow, and that deeper reflection was bound to shew that worse than all conceivable devil-deities is a blind, deaf, dumb, heartless, senseless mob of forces that strike as a tree does when it is blown down by the wind, or as the tree itself is struck by lightning. That did not occur to the humanitarians at the moment: people do not reflect deeply when they are in the first happiness of escape from an intolerably oppressive situation. Like Bunyan's pilgrim they could not see the wicket gate, nor the Slough of Despond, nor the castle of Giant Despair; but they saw the shining light at the end of the path, and so started gaily towards it as Evolutionists.

And they were right; for the problem of evil yields very easily to Creative Evolution. If the driving power behind Evolution is omnipotent only in the sense that there seems no limit to its final achievement; and if it must meanwhile struggle with matter and circumstance by the method of trial and error, then the world must be full of its unsuccessful experiments. Christ may meet a tiger, or a High Priest arm-in-arm with a Roman Governor, and be the unfittest to survive under the circumstances. Mozart may have a genius that prevails against Emperors and Archbishops, and a lung that succumbs to some obscure and noxious property of foul air. If all our calamities are either accidents or sincerely repented mistakes, there is no malice in the Cruelty of Nature and no Problem of Evil in the Victorian sense at all. The theology of the women who told us that they became atheists when they sat by the cradles of their children and saw them strangled by the hand of God is succeeded by the theology of Blanco Posnet, with his 'It was early days when He made the croup, I guess. It was the best He could think of then; but when it turned out wrong on His hands He made you and me to fight the croup for Him.'

How One Touch of Darwin Makes the Whole World Kin

Another humanitarian interest in Darwinism was that Darwin popularized Evolution generally, as well as making his own special contribution to it. Now the general conception of Evolution provides the humanitarian with a scientific basis, because it establishes the fundamental equality of all living things. It makes the killing of an animal murder in exactly the same sense as the killing of a man is murder. It is sometimes necessary to kill men as it is always necessary to kill tigers; but the old theoretic distinction between the two acts has been obliterated by Evolution. When I was a child and was told that our dog and our parrot, with whom I was on intimate terms, were not creatures like myself, but were brutal whilst I was reasonable, I not only did not believe it, but quite consciously and intellectually formed the opinion that the distinction was false; so that afterwards, when Darwin's views were first unfolded to me, I promptly said that I had found out all that for myself before I was ten years old; and I am far from sure that my youthful arrogance was not justified; for this sense of the kinship of all forms of life is all that is needed to make Evolution not only a conceivable theory, but an inspiring one. St Anthony was ripe for the Evolution theory when he preached to the fishes, and St Francis when he called the birds his little brothers. Our vanity, and our snobbish conception of God-head as being, like earthly kingship, a supreme class distinction instead of the rock on which Equality is built, had led us to insist on God offering us special terms by placing us apart from and above all the rest of his creatures. Evolution took that conceit out of us; and now, though we may kill a flea without the smallest remorse, we at all events know that we are killing our cousin. No doubt it shocks the flea when the creature that an almighty Celestial Flea created expressly for the food of fleas, destroys the jumping lord of creation with his sharp and enormous thumbnail; but no flea will ever be so foolish as to preach that in slaying fleas Man is applying a method of Natural Selection which will finally evolve a flea so swift that no man can catch him, and so hardy of constitution that Insect Powder will have no more effect on him than strychnine on an elephant.

[Shaw goes on to explain how the notion of 'Circum-stantial Selection' was a handy one, and carried over into politics, economics, and finance, tending to remove any trace of morality from reasoning in these fields. There has been, however, a 'homeopathic reaction' against Dar-winism.]

The Danger of Reaction

And here arises the danger that when we realize this we shall do just what we did half a century ago, and what Pliable did in The Pilgrim's Progress when Christian landed him in the Slough of Despond: that is, run back in terror to our old superstitions. We jumped out of the frying-pan into the fire; and we are just as likely to jump back again, now that we feel hotter than ever. History records very little in the way of mental activity on the part of the mass of mankind except a series of stampedes from affirmative errors into negative ones and back again. It must therefore be said very precisely and clearly that the bankruptcy of Darwinism does not mean that Nobodaddy was Somebodaddy *with* 'body, parts, and passions' after all; that the world was made in the year 4004 B.C.; that damnation means an eternity of blazing brimstone; that the Immaculate Conception means that sex is sinful and that Christ was parthenogenetically brought forth by a virgin descended in like manner from a line of virgins right back to Eve; that the Trinity is an anthropomorphic monster with three heads which are yet only one head; that in Rome the bread and wine on the altar become flesh and blood, and in England, in a still more mystical manner, they do and they do not; that the Bible is an infallible scientific manual, an accurate historical chronicle, and a complete guide to conduct; that we may lie and cheat and murder and then wash ourselves innocent in the blood of the lamb on Sunday at the cost of a *credo* and a penny in the plate, and so on and so forth. Civilization cannot be saved by people not only crude enough to believe these things, but irreligious enough to believe that such belief constitutes a religion. The education of children cannot safely be left in their hands. If dwindling sects like the Church of England, the Church of Rome, the Greek

Church, and the rest, persist in trying to cramp the human mind within the limits of these grotesque perversions of natural truths and poetic metaphors, then they must be ruthlessly banished from the schools until they either perish in general contempt or discover the soul that is hidden in every dogma. The real Class War will be a war of intellectual classes; and its conquest will be the souls of the children.

A Touchstone for Dogma

The test of a dogma is its universality. As long as the Church of England preaches a single doctrine that the Brahman, the Buddhist, the Mussulman, the Parsee, and all the other sectarians who are British subjects cannot accept, it has no legitimate place in the counsels of the British Commonwealth, and will remain what it is at present, a corrupter of youth, a danger to the State, and an obstruction to the Fellowship of the Holy Ghost. This has never been more strongly felt than at present, after a war in which the Church failed grossly in the courage of its profession, and sold its lilies for the laurels of the soldiers of the Victoria Cross. All the cocks in Christendom have been crowing shame on it ever since; and it will not be spared for the sake of the two or three faithful who were found even among the bishops. Let the Church take it on authority, even my authority (as a professional legend maker) if it cannot see the truth by its own light: no dogma can be a legend. A legend can pass an ethnical frontier as a legend, but not as a truth; whilst the only frontier to the currency of a sound dogma as such is the frontier of capacity for understanding it.

This does not mean that we should throw away legend and parable and drama: they are the natural vehicles of dogma; but woe to the Churches and rulers who substitute the legend for the dogma, the parable for the history, the drama for the religion! Better by far declare the throne of God empty than set a liar and a fool on it. What are called wars of religion are always wars to destroy religion by affirming the historical truth or material substantiality of some legend, and killing those who refuse to accept it as historical or substantial. But who has ever refused to accept a good legend with delight *as* a legend? The legends, the parables, the dramas, are among the choicest treasures of mankind. No one is ever tired of stories of miracles. . . .

What to do with the Legends

What we should do, then, is to pool our legends and make a delightful stock of religious folk-lore on an honest basis for all mankind. With our minds freed from pretence and falsehood we could enter into the heritage of all the faiths. China would share her sages with Spain, and Spain her saints with China. The Ulster man who now gives his son an unmerciful thrashing if the boy is so tactless as to ask how the evening and the morning could be the first day before the sun was created, or to betray an innocent calf-love for the Virgin Mary, would buy him a bookful of legends of the creation and of mothers of God from all parts of the world, and be very glad to find his laddie as interested in such things as in marbles or Police and Robbers. That would be better than beating all good feeling towards religion out of the child, and blackening his mind by teaching him that the worshippers of the holy virgins, whether of the Parthenon or St Peter's, are fire-doomed heathens and idolaters. All the sweetness of religion is conveyed to the world by the hands of story-tellers and image-makers. Without their fictions the truths of religion would for the multitude be neither intelligible nor even apprehensible; and the prophets would prophesy and the teachers teach in vain. And nothing stands between the people and the fictions except the silly falsehood that the fictions are literal truths, and that there is nothing in religion but fiction.

* * *

The Religious Art of the Twentieth Century

Creative Evolution is already a religion, and is indeed now unmistakeably the religion of the twentieth century, newly arisen from the ashes of pseudo-Christianity, of mere scepticism, and of the soulless affirmations and blind negations of the Mechanists and Neo-Darwinians. But it cannot become a popular religion until it has its legends, its parables, its miracles. And when I say popular I do not mean apprehensible by villagers only. I mean apprehensible by Cabinet Ministers as well. It is unreasonable to look to the professional politician and administrator for light and leading in religion. He is neither a philosopher nor a prophet: if he were, he would be philosophizing and prophesying, and not neglecting both for the drudgery of practical government. . . . Your front bench man will always be an exploiter of the popular religion or irreligion. Not being an expert, he must take it as he finds it; and before he can take it, he must have been told stories about it in his childhood and had before him all his life an elaborate iconography of it produced by writers, painters, sculptors, temple architects, and artists of all the higher sorts. Even if, as sometimes happens, he is a bit of an amateur in metaphysics as well as a professional politician, he must still govern according to the popular iconography, and not according to his own personal interpretations if these happen to be heterodox.

It will be seen then that the revival of religion on a scientific basis does not mean the death of art, but a glorious rebirth of it. Indeed art has never been great when it was not providing an iconography for a live religion. And it has never been quite contemptible except when imitating the iconography after the religion had become a superstition. Italian painting from Giotto to Carpaccio is all religious painting; and it moves us deeply and has real greatness. Compare with it the attempts of our painters a century ago to achieve the effects of the old masters by imitation when they should have been illustrating a faith of their own. Contemplate, if you can bear it, the dull daubs of Hilton and Haydon, who knew so much more about drawing and scumbling and glazing and perspective and anatomy and 'marvellous foreshortening' than Giotto, the latchet of whose shoe they were nevertheless not worthy to unloose. Compare Mozart's Magic Flute, Beethoven's Ninth Symphony, Wagner's Ring, all of them reachings-forward to the new Vitalist art, with the dreary pseudo-sacred oratorios and cantatas which were produced for no better reason than that Handel had formerly made splendid thunder in that way, and with the stale confectionery, mostly too would-be pious to be even cheerfully toothsome, of Spohr and Mendelssohn, Stainer and Parry, which spread indigestion at our musical festivals until I publicly told Parry the bludgeoning truth about his Job and woke him to conviction of sin. Compare Flaxman and Thorwaldsen and Gibson with Phidias and Praxiteles, Stevens with Michael Angelo, Bouguereau's Virgin with Cimabue's, or the best operatic Christs of Scheffer and Müller with the worst Christs that the worst painters could paint before the end of the fifteenth century, and you must feel that until we have a great religious movement we cannot hope for a great artistic one. The disillusioned Raphael could paint a mother and child, but not a queen of Heaven as much less skilful men had done in the days of his great-grandfather; yet he could reach forward to the twentieth century and paint a Transfiguration of the Son of Man as they could not. Also, please note, he could decorate a house of pleasure for a cardinal very beautifully with voluptuous pictures of Cupid and Psyche; for this simple sort of Vitalism is always with us, and, like portrait painting, keeps the artist supplied with subject-matter in the intervals between the ages of faith; so that your sceptical Rembrandts and Velasquezs are at least not compelled to paint shop fronts for want of anything else to paint in which they can really believe.

The Artist-Prophets

And there are always certain rare but intensely interesting anticipations. Michael Angelo could not very well believe in Julius II or Leo X, or in much that they believed in; but he could paint the Superman three hundred years before Nietzsche wrote Also Sprach Zarathustra and Strauss set it to music. Michael Angelo won the primacy among all modern painters and sculptors solely by his power of shewing us superhuman persons. On the strength of his decoration and colour alone he would hardly have survived his own death twenty years; and even his design would have had only an academic interest; but as a painter of prophets and sibyls he is greatest among the very greatest in his craft, because we aspire to a world of prophets and sibyls. Beethoven never heard of radio-activity nor of electrons dancing in vortices of inconceivable energy; but pray can anyone explain the last movement of his Hammerklavier Sonata, Opus 106, otherwise than as a musical picture of these whirling electrons? . . .

In Beethoven's day the business of art was held to be 'the

sublime and beautiful'. In our day it has fallen to be the imitative and voluptuous. In both periods the word passionate has been freely employed; but in the eighteenth century passion meant irresistible impulse of the loftiest kind: for example, a passion for astronomy or for truth. For us it has come to mean concupiscence and nothing else. One might say to the art of Europe what Antony said to the corpse of Caesar: 'Are all thy conquests, glories, triumphs, spoils, shrunk to this little measure?' But in fact it is the mind of Europe that has shrunk, being, as we have seen, wholly preoccupied with a busy spring-cleaning to get rid of its superstitions before readjusting itself to the new conception of Evolution.

Evolution in the Theatre

On the stage (and here I come at last to my own particular function in the matter), Comedy, as a destructive, derisory, critical, negative art, kept the theatre open when sublime tragedy perished. From Molière to Oscar Wilde we had a line of comedic playwrights who, if they had nothing fundamentally positive to say, were at least in revolt against falsehood and imposture, and were not only, as they claimed, 'chastening morals by ridicule', but, in Johnson's phrase, clearing our minds of cant, and thereby shewing an uneasiness in the presence of error which is the surest symptom of intellectual vitality. Meanwhile the name of Tragedy was assumed by plays in which everyone was killed in the last act, just as, in spite of Molière, plays in which everyone was married in the last act called themselves comedies. Now neither tragedies nor comedies can be produced according to a prescription which gives only the last moments of the last act. Shakespear did not make Hamlet out of its final butchery, nor Twelfth Night out of its final matrimony. And he could not become the conscious iconographer of a religion because he had no conscious religion. He had therefore to exercise his extraordinary natural gifts in the very entertaining art of mimicry, giving us the famous 'delineation of character' which makes his plays, like the novels of Scott, Dumas, and Dickens, so delightful. Also, he developed that curious and questionable art of building us a refuge from despair by disguising the cruelties of Nature as jokes. But with all his gifts, the fact remains that he never found the inspiration to write an original play. He furbished up old plays, and adapted popular stories, and chapters of history from Holinshed's Chronicle and Plutarch's biographies, to the stage. All this he did (or did not; for there are minus quantities in the algebra of art) with a recklessness which shewed that his trade lay far from his conscience. It is true that he never takes his characters from the borrowed story, because it was less trouble and more fun to him to create them afresh; but none the less he heaps the murders and villainies of the borrowed story on his own essentially gentle creations without scruple, no matter how incongruous they may be. And all the time his vital need for a philosophy drives him to seek one by the quaint professional method of introducing philosophers as characters into his plays, and even of making his heroes philosophers; but when they come on the stage they have no philosophy to expound: they are only pessimists and railers; and their occasional would-be philosophic speeches, such as The Seven Ages of Man and The Soliloquy on Suicide, shew how deeply in the dark Shakespear was as to what philosophy means. He forced himself in among the greatest of playwrights without having once entered that region in which Michael Angelo, Beethoven, Goethe, and the antique Athenian stage poets are great. He would really not be great at all if it were not that he had religion enough to be aware that his religionless condition was one of despair. His towering King Lear would be only a melodrama were it not for its express admission that if there is nothing more to be said of the universe than Hamlet has to say, then 'as flies to wanton boys are we to the gods: they kill us for their sport'.

Ever since Shakespear, playwrights have been struggling with the same lack of religion; and many of them were forced to become mere panders and sensation-mongers because, though they had higher ambitions, they could find no better subject-matter. From Congreve to Sheridan they were so sterile in spite of their wit that they did not achieve between them the output of Molière's single lifetime; and they were all (not without reason) ashamed of their profession, and preferred to be regarded as mere men of fashion with a rakish hobby. Goldsmith's was the only saved soul in that pandemonium.

The leaders among my own contemporaries (now veterans) snatched at minor social problems rather than write entirely without any wider purpose than to win money and fame. One of them expressed to me his envy of the ancient Greek playwrights because the Athenians asked them, not for some 'new and original' disguise of the half-dozen threadbare plots of the modern theatre, but for the deepest lesson they could draw from the familiar and sacred legends of their country. 'Let us all,' he said, 'write an Electra, an Antigone, an Agamemnon, and shew what we can do with it.' But he did not write any of them, because these legends are no longer religious: Aphrodite and Artemis and Poseidon are deader than their statues. . . . The giants of the theatre of our time, Ibsen and Strindberg, had no greater comfort for the world than we: indeed much less; for they refused us even the Shakespearean–Dickensian consolation of laughter at mischief, accurately called comic relief. Our emancipated young successors scorn us, very properly. But they will be able to do no better whilst the drama remains pre-Evolutionist. Let them consider the great exception of Goethe. He, no richer than Shakespear, Ibsen, or Strindberg in specific talent as a playwright, is in the empyrean whilst they are gnashing their teeth in impotent fury in the mud, or at best finding an acid enjoyment in the irony of their predicament. Goethe is Olympian: the other giants are infernal in everything but their veracity and their repudiation of the irreligion of their time: that is, they are bitter and hopeless. It is not a question of mere dates. Goethe was an Evolutionist in 1830: many playwrights, even young ones, are still untouched by Creative Evolution in 1920. Ibsen was Darwinized to the extent of exploiting heredity on the stage much as the ancient Athenian playwrights exploited the Eumenides; but there is no trace in his plays of any faith in or knowledge of Creative Evolution as a modern scientific fact. True, the poetic aspiration is plain enough in his Emperor or Galilean; but it is one of Ibsen's distinctions that nothing was valid for him but science; and he left that vision of the future which his Roman seer calls 'the third Empire' behind him as a Utopian dream when he settled down to his serious grapple with realities in those plays of modern life with which he overcame Europe, and broke the dusty windows of every dry-rotten theatre in it from Moscow to Manchester.

My Own Part in the Matter

In my own activities as a playwright I found this state of things intolerable. The fashionable theatre prescribed one serious subject: clandestine adultery: the dullest of all subjects for a serious author, whatever it may be for audiences who read the police intelligence and skip the reviews and leading articles. I tried slum-landlordism, doctrinaire Free Love (pseudo-Ibsenism), prostitution, militarism, marriage, history, current politics, natural Christianity, national and individual character, paradoxes of conventional society, husband hunting, questions of conscience, professional delusions and impostures, all worked into a series of comedies of manners in the classic fashion, which was then very much out of fashion, the mechanical tricks of Parisian 'construction' being *de rigueur* in the theatre. But this, though it occupied me and established me professionally, did not constitute me an iconographer of the religion of my time, and thus fulfil my natural function as an artist. I was quite conscious of this; for I had always known that civilization needs a religion as a matter of life or death; and as the conception of Creative Evolution developed I saw that we were at last within reach of a faith which complied with the first condition of all the religions that have ever taken hold of humanity: namely, that it must be, first and fundamentally, a science of metabiology. This was a crucial point with me; for I had seen Bible fetishism, after standing up to all the rationalistic batteries of Hume, Voltaire, and the rest, collapse before the onslaught of much less gifted Evolutionists, solely because they discredited it as a biological document; so that from that moment it lost its hold, and left literate Christendom faithless. My own Irish eighteenth-centuryism made it impossible for me to believe anything until I could conceive it as a scientific hypothesis, even though the abominations, quackeries, impostures, venalities, credulities, and delusions of the camp followers of science, and the brazen lies and priestly pretensions of the pseudo-scientific cure-mongers, all sedulously inculcated by modern 'secondary education', were so monstrous that I was sometimes forced to make a verbal distinction between science and knowledge lest I should mislead my readers. But I never forgot that without knowledge even wisdom is more dangerous than mere opportunist ignorance, and that somebody must take the Garden of Eden in hand and weed it properly.

Accordingly, in 1901, I took the legend of Don Juan in its Mozartian form and made it a dramatic parable of Creative Evolution. But being then at the height of my invention and comedic talent, I decorated it too brilliantly and lavishly. . . .

I now find myself inspired to make a second legend of Creative Evolution without distractions and embellishments. My sands are running out; the exuberance of 1901 has aged into the garrulity of 1920; and the war has been a stern intimation that the matter is not one to be trifled with. I abandon the legend of Don Juan with its erotic associations, and go back to the legend of the Garden of Eden. I exploit the eternal interest of the philosopher's stone which enables men to live for ever. I am not, I hope, under more illusion than is humanly inevitable as to the crudity of this my beginning of a Bible for Creative Evolution. I am doing the best I can at my age. My powers are waning; but so much the better for those who found me unbearably brilliant when I was in my prime. It is my hope that a hundred apter and more elegant parables by younger hands will soon leave mine as far behind as the religious pictures of the fifteenth century left behind the first attempts of the early Christians at iconography. In that hope I withdraw and ring up the curtain.

[1920]

Back to Methuselah

After dramatizing the stages by which men may evolve from the birth of their knowledge in the Garden of Eden to the bodiless form of pure intellect in 'As Far as Thought Can Reach', the playwright pauses at the end of his major opus to let the spirits of Adam, Eve, Cain, the Serpent, and Lilith survey the panorama of life which they had begun, and which seems to have no end.

Lilith becomes visible between Cain and Adam.

LILITH. I suffered unspeakably; I tore myself asunder; I lost my life, to make of my one flesh these twain, man and woman. And this is what has come of it. What do you make of it, Adam, my son?

ADAM. I made the earth bring forth by my labour, and the woman bring forth by my love. And this is what has come of it. What do you make of it, Eve, my wife?

EVE. I nourished the egg in my body and fed it with my blood. And now they let it fall as the birds did, and suffer not at all. What do you make of it, Cain, my first-born?

CAIN. I invented killing and conquest and mastery and the winnowing out of the weak by the strong. And now the strong have slain one another; and the weak live for ever; and their deeds do nothing for the doer more than for another. What do you make of it, snake?

THE SERPENT. I am justified. For I chose wisdom and the knowledge of good and evil; and now there is no evil; and wisdom and good are one. It is enough. [*She vanishes.*]

CAIN. There is no place for me on earth any longer. You cannot deny that mine was a splendid game while it lasted. But now! Out, out, brief candle! [*He vanishes.*]

EVE. The clever ones were always my favourites. The diggers and the fighters have dug themselves in with the worms. My clever ones have inherited the earth. All's well. [*She fades away.*]

ADAM. I can make nothing of it, neither head nor tail. What is it all for? Why? Whither? Whence? We were well enough in the garden. And now the fools have killed all the animals; and they are dissatisfied because they cannot be bothered with their bodies! Foolishness, I call it. [*He disappears.*]

LILITH. They have accepted the burden of eternal life. They have taken the agony from birth; and their life does not fail them even in the hour of their destruction. Their breasts are without milk: their bowels are gone: the very shapes of them are only ornaments for their children to admire and caress without understanding. Is this enough; or shall I labour again? Shall I bring forth something that will sweep them away and make an end of them as they have swept away the beasts of the garden, and made an end of the crawling things and the flying things and of all them that refuse to live for ever? I had patience with them for many ages: they tried me very sorely. They did terrible things: they embraced death, and said that eternal life was a fable. I stood amazed at the malice and destructiveness of the things I had made: Mars blushed as he looked down on the shame of his sister planet: cruelty and hypocrisy became so hideous that the face of the earth was pitted with the graves of little children among which living skeletons

125

SHAW ON RELIGION

crawled in search of horrible food. The pangs of another birth were already upon me when one man repented and lived three hundred years; and I waited to see what would come of that. And so much came of it that the horrors of that time seem now but an evil dream. They have redeemed themselves from their vileness, and turned away from their sins. Best of all, they are still not satisfied: the impulse I gave them in that day when I sundered myself in twain and launched Man and Woman on the earth still urges them: after passing a million goals they press on to the goal of redemption from the flesh, to the vortex freed from matter, to the whirlpool in pure intelligence that, when the world began, was a whirlpool in pure force. And though all that they have done seems but the first hour of the infinite work of creation, yet I will not supersede them until they have forded this last stream that lies between flesh and spirit, and disentangled their life from the matter that has always mocked it. I can wait: waiting and patience mean nothing to the eternal. I gave the woman the greatest of gifts: curiosity. By that her seed has been saved from my wrath; for I also am curious; and I have waited always to see what they will do tomorrow. Let them feed that appetite well for me. I say, let them dread, of all things, stagnation; for from the moment I, Lilith, lose hope and faith in them, they are doomed. In that hope and faith I have let them live for a moment; and in that moment I have spared them many times. But mightier creatures than they have killed hope and faith, and perished from the earth; and I may not spare them for ever. I am Lilith: I brought life into the whirlpool of force, and compelled my enemy, Matter, to obey a living soul. But in enslaving Life's enemy I made him Life's master; for that is the end of all slavery; and now I shall see the slave set free and the enemy reconciled, the whirlpool become all life and no matter. And because these

126

infants that call themselves ancients are reaching out towards that, I will have patience with them still; though I
know well that when they attain it they shall become one
with me and supersede me, and Lilith will be only a legend
and a lay that has lost its meaning. Of Life only is there no
end; and though of its million starry mansions many are
empty and many still unbuilt, and though its vast domain
is as yet unbearably desert, my seed shall one day fill it and
master its matter to its uttermost confines. And for what
may be beyond, the eyesight of Lilith is too short. It is
enough that there is a beyond. [*She vanishes.*]

[1920]

A Catechism on My Creed

The Dean referred to near the end of this sprightly interview was William Ralph Inge (1860–1954), Dean of St Paul's after 1905, whom Shaw has referred to elsewhere as 'a Platonist Quaker'.

The 'Catechism' appeared in the *St. Martin-in-the-Fields Review* for May 1922. The 'Catechist' was Margaret Ponsonby.

Do you believe (a) That there must be 'somebody behind the something'? (b) In a First Cause? (c) That the universe made itself and that our world is a pure accident?

(*a*) No: I believe that there is something behind the somebody. All bodies are products of the Life Force (whatever that may be); and to put the body behind the thing that made it is to reverse the order of Nature, and also to violate the first article of the Church of England, which expressly declares that God has neither body, parts, nor passions.

(*b*) A First Cause is a contradiction in terms, because in Causation every cause must have a cause; and therefore there can no more be a First Cause than a first inch in a circle. If you once admit a cause that is uncaused, you give up Causation altogether. And if you do that, you may as well say that everything makes itself. But it can only do that if it is alive; so you are back again at your mystery, and may as well confess that to your ignorance and limited faculty the universe is unaccountable. I daresay every black-beetle thinks it must have a complete explanation of the world as one of the indispensable qualifications of a respect-able cockroach; but it will have to do without it for a while yet.

(c) All life is a series of accidents; but when you find most of them pointing all one way, you may guess that there is something behind them that is not accidental.

Do you believe that given enough data to go on we could account for everything?
No. As a matter of fact we have data enough, from the Alps to the electrons, to account for everything fifty times over; but we have not the brains to interpret them.

You think the Church has 'failed grossly in the courage of its profession', and therefore you disbelieve in it. But the Labour Party has equally missed its opportunity, yet you believe in it. Why?
The Church has failed infamously: I can hardly imagine how it has the face to exist after its recreancy during the war. But what has that to do with belief or disbelief? The Church of England is only a Society of gentlemen amateurs, half of them pretending to be properly trained and dis-ciplined priests, and the other half pretending that they are breezy public schoolboys with no parsonic nonsense about them. They profess to sustain and propagate religious faith; but their failure or success, their honesty or dishonesty, their sense or their folly, cannot affect the faith: it can only affect the attendance in the buildings in which they pontificate. If a man sells me a bad motor car, I can take my custom away from him, and denounce him as an imposter, without ceasing to believe in the science of mechanics. There are

churches where the parson snarls the service and bullies God like a barrister at the Old Bailey. There are churches where he is a duffer, and churches where he is a snob. But that does not prevent people going to St Martin's. The Church is what the parsons make it; and when a man says he does not hold with the Church, and that parsons are frauds, we generally find either that he never goes to church, or else that his particular parson *is* a fraud. The same thing is true of the Labour Party. It, also, is what the Labour men make it. But the truths it stands for remain none the less true.

Do you agree with Voltaire who said 'To believe in God is impossible, not to believe in him is absurd'?

No. Voltaire's remark was witty – that is, true – when he made it; and it is still true of the Omnipotent Personality, with body, parts, and passions, which the word God meant in Voltaire's time. But our God, the God who is still struggling with the work of Creative Evolution, and using us as his labourers, having created us for the purpose, and proceeding by the method of trial and error, presents no such difficulty. Unfortunately, many of our people have not yet caught up with Voltaire, much less with the twentieth century; and for them it would be a considerable advance if they were to become Voltaireans.

What effect do you think it would have on the country if every Church were shut and every parson unfrocked? Do you think a Religion is a necessity for the development of a nation? and if so, must it not have some organization for its development? Or do you believe that nothing can be organized in the realm of the Spirit in this present existence?

A very salutary effect indeed. It would soon provoke an irresistible demand for the Re-establishment of the Church, which could then start again without the superstitions that make it so impossible today. At present the Church has to make itself cheap in all sorts of ways to induce people to attend its services; and the cheaper it makes itself the less the people attend. Its articles are out of date; its services are out of date; and its ministers are men to whom such things do not matter because they are out of date themselves. The marriage service and the burial service are unbearable to people who take them seriously – and please do not conclude that I am thinking now of the current foolish and prudish objections to the sensible and true parts of the marriage service. Your main point is what would happen if the people suddenly found themselves without churches and rituals. So many of them would find that they had been deprived of a necessity of life that the want would have to be supplied; and there would presently be more churches than ever, and fuller ones. The only people who can do without churches are the simple materialists on the one hand, and on the other those who have no use for institutional worship because their churches are their own souls. That is the Quaker position; but you find such people in all circles. They are sometimes artists, sometimes philosophers; and the irony of circumstance has landed one of them in the extraordinary predicament of being a Dean.

Do you think Christ is still a living influence in the present day?

Yes; but there are, as he expected there would be, a good many very unchristlike people trading under his name: for instance, St. Paul. The wholesale rebellion against Christ's teaching which culminated in the war has turned out so very badly that just at present there are probably more people who feel that in him is the only hope for the world than there ever were before in the lifetime of men now living.

[1922]

131

The Infancy of God

This hitherto unpublished essay was apparently written especially for inclusion in the abandoned religious volume of the Collected Works. In essence it states the theme which Nickles echoed a generation later in Archibald MacLeish's *J.B.*:

> 'If God is God He is not good,
> If God is good He is not God.'

The exact date of writing is uncertain.

I wish at the outset to clear myself of all suspicion of that confusion of religion with Veneration which enables most men to imagine themselves religious when they are only reverent. I am myself, and always have been, as religious a man as Voltaire; but as I have also been, like him, an extremely irreverent one, most Englishmen are unable to conceive me as religious. I have no power to alter this state of things. Many years ago I found myself in a vegetarian restaurant in Barbican, sitting opposite a man who began to discuss religion with me. Before I had at all shewn my hand on the subject, he said: 'I can see you are a sceptic.' 'How do you know?' said I. 'I am a bit of a phrenologist,' said he. 'Oh,' said I, 'have I no bump of veneration?' 'Bump of veneration!' he exclaimed: 'Why, it's a hole.' And as a matter of fact that part of the scalp which in very devout worshippers and very obedient moralists rises into a dome or a ridge like a church roof, is on my scalp a majestic plain with a slight depression in the centre.

To ask me to be reverent, with whatever moving appeals to good taste, is like asking me to hang from a tree by my tail. In me nature has discarded the tail, having higher uses for me than hanging on trees upside down. She has also discarded the bump of veneration, having nobler attitudes for me than kneeling and grovelling. I have achieved at least one of the characteristics of the Superman: the upright posture of the soul; and I am as proud of it as the first monkey who achieved the upright posture of the body, and so felt himself a stage nearer the Supermonkey, man.

Yet I am not so far evolved that I cannot understand veneration. It is important that every statesman (and I write always for statesmen) should know that veneration is a passion; and that its satisfaction brings a comfort so ineffable that its voluptuaries never stop to think out what it implies, and are consequently not degraded by it as they would be if they had thought it out – as I should be by it, for example. Let me think it out for the purpose of this book, on paper. To venerate, you must have something higher than yourself before you. To obtain the utmost satisfaction for your passion of veneration, you conceive a God who is omnipotent, omniscient, and infinitely good. And you think no more about it, but worship and are happy. But I, having no such use for this ideal, and having, instead, an instinct for criticism, immediately begin to reflect. I see that the veneration scheme implies that an all-powerful God, to whom nothing is impossible, has deliberately created something lower than himself for the sake of enjoying his own superiority to them, just as a snob surrounds himself with footmen or an unkingly king with flatterers.

Immediately my chin goes up; and my back stiffens. I, with all my faults and follies, am at least better than this; for, being man, I strive to surpass myself and produce Superman; whilst this God of the people with ridged and domed heads, does not try to produce a Supergod, but produces subgods, giving them all sorts of ridiculous and disastrous weaknesses so that he may despise them. This God will not do for me at all: to be quite frank, I consider him a cad. Unless I can bring you to the knowledge of some higher divinity than that, I may as well shut up my treatise on religion, and write farces.

Yet such a God is at present indispensable to the statesman, and, as I have said, to the venerators also. To the statesman, because the ridged and domed men, of whom there are many, will not obey laws or officials through a comprehension of the need for subordinators, but only through veneration for the lawgiver and the official. To induce them to do anything subordinate, you have to set up a golden calf for them to adore, and persuade them that your officials are its ministers, to which end you must deck the officials in the best trappings your stage managers can devise, and set them apart by every device of caste and money that can make them appear awful and venerable. And you will find the task a very easy one; for the passion of veneration is so strong that the ridged heads and what Shakespear called the pregnant knees will bend and crook before the most pitiful and grotesque makeshifts. Humanity has not yet produced a creature so cruel, so disgusting, so silly, or even so common, but it will find adorers as loyal as the noblest kings and bishops known to history. Just as the amorous voluptuary soon comes to care nothing for the lover and everything for the passion, so the ridged and domed care everything for loyalty and piety and nothing for the king or bishop. Nero will serve their turn as well as Alfred.

The blacking on the shoes of 'Great Catherine, whom the world still adores' is as sweet to their lips as that on the shoes of the virgin Elizabeth. Neither their loyalty nor their devotion affords the smallest guarantee of good government or lofty religion. It guarantees nothing but its idol; and if its idol deepens the emotional effect from time to time by some appalling crime, his hold is all the surer; the cult of pleasure is near akin to the cult of pain. What finally wrecks all republics, and is now struggling fiercely with Democracy, is this Idolatry, abhorred of all the prophets. The English Commonwealth of the XVII century failed because it starved the idolator; it took away his king and his bishop; and Cromwell, had he lived, would have had to crown himself or perish; for he could not have gone on much longer with his armed heel on the throat of an idolatrous nation without pretending that he was something more than a man of like passions to themselves.

Democracy is fundamentally a proposal that we should live without idols, obeying laws and doing justly because we understand the need for doing so, and making an end of purely lascivious veneration and idolatry. In every democratic revolution the democrats instinctively begin by rushing to the cathedral and knocking off the heads of the statues. It then proceeds to the residences of the human idols – the official persons – and knocks off their heads also. When, as often happens, these unlucky living idols are excellent functionaries and estimable, kindly, or at worst quite commonplace individuals, such acts of mob violence seem as senseless as they are cruel. Even those who care little about the slaughter of men are infuriated by the destruction of priceless works of art. All the same, there must be some logic in the action of a thousand men who all do the same thing without stopping to paralyse thousands with inept arguing. In Paris, in 1789, there was not in the Bastille a single prisoner about whom the mob cared a rap; and the governor was no worse a man than any other military gentleman with a good place. But when the mob demolished the Bastille and hacked off Delaunay's head, they were demonstrating that the Bastille was only a heap of stones and its governor only a man who would die when you cut his throat: a demonstration which had been made necessary by the success with which the Bastille had been imposed on France as the inviolate temple of a terrible and irresistible idol called the King, and the Governor as a High Priest wielding the idol's power vicariously. In the same way, if no one had ever thought Charles I more than a man, Cromwell would never have taken the trouble to prove that his neck, at all events, was mortal, and that one could shear through it without being struck by lightning. And when Cromwell, having in due course become something of an idol, was dug out of his grave and hung up in chains, that, too, was thought necessary to shew people that what he had done was no more than any common criminal could have done. It is but a few years since, in the Sudan, we desecrated the tomb of the Mahdi, and mutilated his corpse to prove that Mahomet would not avenge him; and no doubt we shall yet see the statue of Gordon we set up in his place duly defiled and decapitated by the next Mahometan conqueror to prove that it, too, is under no special supernatural protection.

All these tides of idolatry and iconoclasm are to me, and therefore presumably to many other people, stupid and disgusting. To us idolatry, though easy, and, for the mere mechanical purposes of law and order, effective, is a rotten and degrading basis for society, and reduces religion to 'a rhapsody of words', as Shakespear put it. We want intelligent obedience instead of idolatrous obedience, as that is our only guarantee against the abuse of power for the private ends of those whom we must trust with it.

So far, this is mere political commonplace. The need for political intelligence in order to secure rebellion the moment our governors betray their trust has been demonstrated quite often enough, in spite of the fact that the Ridged and Domed remain constitutionally impervious to it. What has been less noticed is the danger that arises from the fact that idolators always expect too much from their idols, and in the fury of their disappointment often outdo the iconoclasts when an insurrection is provoked by famine or defeat. Anatole France tells the story of a peasant who, praying before a statue of the Virgin and Child, addressed the latter in these terms: 'It is not to thee, son of a wanton, that I offer my prayer, but to thy sainted mother.' On a previous occasion he had made his petition to the Infant Christ without success; and when it was not granted he abused the obdurate deity just as Russian peasants, when they have prayed in vain for good weather to their Ikons, take them into the fields and beat them.

We have the same phenomenon in politics, where it takes the form of 'the swing of the pendulum' at general elections. Our Party leaders are idolized. The inevitable consequence is that impossibilities are expected from them. They are held accountable for the harvests, for the fluctuations of trade, for the fortune of war, for every private mishap and every public calamity, whilst at the same time they get no credit for beneficial measures that are beyond the comprehension of their idolators. Consequently they are thrown down and smashed, and the Opposition set up on their pedestals and worshipped until the pendulum swings again, when they are set up again and given another turn. At last the governing classes become entirely cynical as to democracy and set themselves deliberately to perfect themselves in the art of exploiting idolatry.

This also is something of a commonplace as far as politics

are concerned. But its application to religion is less familiar. How about the man who expects too much from his God?

How are atheists produced? In probably nine cases out of ten, what happens is something like this. A beloved wife or husband or child or sweetheart is gnawed to death by cancer, stultified by epilepsy, struck dumb and helpless by apoplexy, or strangled by croup or diphtheria; and the looker-on, after praying vainly to God to refrain from such horrible and wanton cruelty, indignantly repudiates faith in the divine monster, and becomes not merely indifferent and sceptical, but fiercely and actively hostile to religion. This result is inevitable when once the level is passed beneath which idolatry is intensified by cruelty. For all people are not driven from religion by calamity: many are driven just the other way by it. Whilst their circumstances are happy they never think of religion; but 'plague, pestilence and famine, battle, murder, and sudden death' impress them with such a dread of the majesty and power of God, that they spend the rest of their lives in worship and propitiation. It is the stronger spirits, the thinkers, those with a high ideal of God and the power and courage to criticize and judge God by the standard of that high ideal, who revolt against his cruelty, denouncing him as 'the Almighty Fiend' of Shelley; and finally rejecting the tale of his existence as a hideous dream. Although atheism may be mere stupidity, yet the intelligent atheist is generally superior to the average worshipper in intellect, and in character as well. When the Westminster and Fortnightly Reviews were distinctly atheistic reviews, they were as superior to their orthodox competitors in intelligence and culture as the extinct National Reformer and the Freethinker of today to the Parish Magazine. The association of scepticism with high mental gift soon became so firmly established that orthodoxy was a positive disadvantage in a scientific career, a useless qualification in medicine and law, and a thing not to be too strongly insisted on even by clergymen and schoolmasters. The Bishop who reminded people, however unintentionally, of the sceptical abbés of the French salons of the XVIII century, was much more fashionable than any of his evangelical colleagues could hope to be. It became necessary to invent a polite euphemism for the terms atheist and atheism; and we now speak of Agnostics and Agnosticism, representing sometimes, no doubt, an entirely honest confession of ignorance as to the ultimate problems of existence, but mostly the state of mind of those who have neither faith to believe nor courage to deny. But whether the attitude was frankly and boldly negative or timidly non-committal, what was at the back of it in nine cases out of ten was the horror of a God who was not only the God of honour, of love, and of light, but also the God of epilepsy, of cancer, of smallpox, of madness, of war, of poverty, of tyranny: in short, of the huge burden of pain and evil under which the world has always groaned and is still groaning more pitifully than ever. In vain did the orthodox attempt to propitiate the agnostics by throwing over the imaginary hell of everlasting brimstone: they could not throw over the real hell which was flaming all round them. And so, as Nietzsche put it, the news went round that God was dead.

Now this whole difficulty was created by the idolatry which conceives God as perfect and omnipotent. If he is omnipotent, then he is a hopeless puzzle. He is not the Almighty Fiend of Shelley's Queen Mab, because he is also the God of veracity, honour, and kindness. And he is not the God of love and mercy because he is also the god of the tubercle bacillus, and the guilty butt of the sarcasms of Mephistopheles. Now a god who is a puzzle is no use. It is easy to say 'If I could understand him, he would not be a god: how can a creature understand the creator?'; but if you do not understand God, you may as well be an atheist for all practical purposes, because you must leave the thing you do not understand out of account. The moment you make any law or give any counsel on the ground that the thing you enjoin or forbid will please him or offend him, you are pretending to understand him to that extent: that is, you are treating him, not as a puzzle, but as a consistent, understood, ascertained character. And with what assurance can you undertake to say that any given conduct will please or displease a deity who is responsible for all the cruelty and evil of life as well as for all the good? It ends inevitably, as it always has ended, either in ignoring him altogether or making him the excuse for whatever you feel inclined to do, whether it happens to be a crime or a benefaction. The latter course, which prevailed as long as God was exempt from criticism, is now so revolting to the Opposition that God is never mentioned in Parliament, and very seldom out of it, except to give emphasis to an expletive.

In the old times, God was not really conceived as omnipotent, but as the divine antagonist of a malign power which wrestled with him for the souls of men. The Father of Lies and the Author of Evil was not God but Satan, who was so vividly imagined that Luther threw his inkpot at him. Fortunately a malignant god – a devil – is too grotesquely horrible a thing to be believed in. A god with horns and a tail is ridiculous; and a fallen archangel is not really a devil: people began to defend him and make him the hero of the piece instead of the villain.

The moment this point is reached it is all over with the old childish way of accounting for evil as the work of Old Nick the mischief maker. And yet that nurse's tale has made us familiar with a conception of immeasurable value. When he wanted to do anything he had to tempt a man or woman to do it. Failing that instrument, he could do nothing. Now one glance at the world as it exists, or at the pages of history, will shew that this is also the method of God. You may call it inspiration in the one case and temptation in the other, out of politeness to God; but the two things are as identical as steadfastness and obstinacy. When a hungry and penniless man stands between his good and his bad angel in front of a baker's shop, the good angel cannot seize and drag him away, nor can the bad angel thrust the loaf into his hands. The victory of honesty or the consummation of a theft must be effected by the man; and his choice will depend a good deal on the sort of man he is. Not only is he an indispensable agent; not only is he the vehicle of the force that moves him; but he is also the vehicle of the force that chooses. He is, in the old phrase, the temple of the Holy Ghost. He has, in another old phrase, the divine spark within him.

Now, to the extent that a man is the temple of the Holy Ghost and the agent of the Holy Ghost, he is necessarily also the limitation of the Holy Ghost. Not even the Holy Ghost can lift ten pounds with a baby's arm or ten tons with a man's. Not even the divine spark can solve a problem in fluxions with the brain of an actor, or play Hamlet with the brain of a mathematician. When 'the word became flesh' it had to take on all the weaknesses of flesh. In all ages the saints and prophets have had to protest against the demand made on them for miracles. John Bunyan's inspiration could make him write better than Shakespear; but it could not make him write always grammatically. It could nerve Mahomet to convert the fierce tribes of Arabia from worshipping stones to an exalted monotheism; but it could not make him say No to a pretty woman. The sword will snap in the hand of God at just the point at which it will snap in a testing machine; and all the swords of God bend and snap at one point and another, or cut the wrong throats at the bidding of the ape or tiger from whom they are evolved.

Now if God (so to speak) were omnipotent, it is clear that he would provide himself with a perfectly fashioned and trustworthy instrument. And it is also clear that such an instrument would be nothing less than God himself incarnate. The fact that man is his best instrument so far on this planet, and that 999 out of every 1000 men are so stupid and cruel, so clumsy and imbecile, that they drive the thousandth to despair even when they do not murder him in sheer dread and hatred of his superiority, proves that God is as yet only in his infancy.

[192?]

A Note on the Prayer Book

The following 'Note' is also published here for the first time, but it was apparently prepared as a commentary on the proposals of H. R. L. Sheppard, Vicar of the Church of St. Martin-in-the-Fields from 1914 to 1927.

Shaw was in continuous revolt against the remnants of Otherworldliness that clung to the Church and against the doctrine of Original Sin. (*'All* conceptions are immaculate,' he once answered a startled questioner at a lecture.) In this regard it is interesting that he should make passing reference to Pelagius, the fifth-century British monk whose heresy was the belief in man's unaided goodness.

Certain comments from the church of St Martin-in-the-Fields on the Book of Common Prayer have startled the people who have never given the subject five minutes serious consideration, and who are indeed so little interested in the Church that they have been too much occupied with the city news or the sporting news or the fashionable news or the parliamentary news to notice that the demand for the revision of the Prayer Book has been clamorous for many years, and that the work has been actually taken in hand by the Church bodies and has given rise to many heated debates and exciting divisions in the fullest publicity. Now

143

that a beneficed clergyman has reached their consciousness they rise up wailing that the Church is about to be destroyed. But they will soon forget their panic; and when revision is carried out they will never notice it, as the Legend of the Jabberwock and The Dying Christian to His Soul are all the same to them, provided they are read by a surpliced person with occasional diversions on the organ, and relieved by standings up and sittings down with a bout or two of kneeling.

Those to whom the Church ritual and services mean something know that the Prayer Book as it stands is indefensible, and that civil marriage, civil registration, and funerals at which there is either no service at all or one improvised by the friends of the deceased are preferred by many people to Church marriage, baptism, and burial, not because these people are irreligious, but on the contrary because they are too religious to be able, at the most solemn moments of their lives, to bear listening to a clergyman saying things which they do not believe, and which he does not believe unless he is an imbecile in such matters. An example is given by the clerical Revisionist from the marriage service, in which, after receiving from the bridegroom a pledge of life-long monogamy, he has to exhort him to take for his model in domestic conduct a polygamous oriental patriarch; and this illustrates with comic vividness the paralysis of thought which religion produced in the authors of the Prayer Book, and still produces in our worshippers; for though many vulgarly prudish people have objected to the marriage service because it necessarily mentions matters which are taboo at the nursery teatable, I cannot remember anyone before Mr Sheppard pointing out that the household of Abraham, Sarah, and Hagar, if taken seriously and literally as a model of our suburbs, would lead to a multiplication of *ménages à trois*. The polygamy of Salt Lake City

144

was in fact defended by citing the examples of the patriarchs.

But whilst admitting all these points, and some more that my Revisionist friend might have made, the fact remains that it seems almost impossible to bring the Prayer Book into harmony with modern thought without spoiling it. It is saturated from beginning to end with a magical belief in transubstantiation; and it is from this that it derives all its beauty and impressiveness. Take that magic away, and the residue will be as dull as an average ethical tract, which is perhaps the dullest thing on earth. Leave it in, and the service glows, repeatedly with a thrilling and consoling faith, and changes the unbearable void of infinite space into a vision of paradise.

The difficulty is that there is in the human soul an imperative demand for reality which no sweetness of consolation or beauty of vision can satisfy or silence. No matter how beautifully a story is worded or said or sung, if it is only a fairy story its charm will not last; and those who, like Mr Sheppard, have to repeat it again and again, or, like his congregation, listen to it again and again, will finally lose patience with it and demand something real and credible told in terms of their own daily life.

Let me make quite clear what scope I am giving to the word transubstantiation. If I do not, all my readers will assume that I am thinking only of the elements in the Mass, of the bread and wine on the Lord's table. But this is only the very crudest part of the ritual: a curious survival of the practice of the warrior who ate his enemy to acquire his fighting qualities and of the refinement upon it of the Central American who ate his God symbolically to acquire some of his divinity, kept alive by the more subtle doctrine of the Epistle to the Corinthians. Transubstantiation does not mean merely that bread turns into flesh and wine into blood, as they do every day by simple metabolism, but that our corruptible body and mortal flesh and blood, which is such a trouble to us, can be changed by faith into an incorruptible and immortal spiritual body. If this transfiguration and transubstantiation is once accepted as a possibility every consideration beside its achievement sinks into utter insignificance. Our corruptible body with its needs and pleasures becomes an abomination to be cast off at the earliest possible moment, and meanwhile to be despised, mortified, shamed, and held in subjection and contempt, and all the services of the Church have only one object, the preparation for the great change, the hastening of it, and the ritual symbolizing of it. The baptism of the child, though it may incidentally enlist it as Christ's soldier and servant, is essentially to change it symbolically by water and the spirit from an abhorred little bundle of original sin to an immortal and incorruptible child of God. A clergyman who is a natural born Pelagian objects strongly to be compelled to call on a mother to loathe her child's body in this fashion, and would rather read Wordsworth's Intimations of Immortality to her, in which her child is trailing clouds of glory as it comes from God in innocence and loveliness. But if the mother believes in transubstantiation, she will rejoice in the hope that this very troublesome little physical body of her baby, which is by no means to her the exquisite amorino it is to the male painter or poet, can be transfigured into an angel. All the apparent morbidities of the services become reasonable and natural on the basis of this belief; and those who grasp it fully can understand not only why a clergyman has to treat the natural body of the infant he baptizes as a tainted survival of 'the old man', or 'the old Adam', to be exchanged as soon as possible for a more glorious spiritual body: they can also understand how in the first days of the gospel, men were seen by St Augustine blackening their wives' eyes for tempting them, or when they escaped the snare of matrimony, voluntarily lived in bodily filth and misery in caves or on the tops of pillars, chastising and shaming the old Adam so that it might give way the more easily to the new Christ.

But if the Prayer Book stands with transubstantiation, it also falls with it. As long as we believe in transubstantiation the Prayer Book will be sacred to us; and we shall overlook such slips as the one about Abraham sooner than suffer anyone to lay a finger on it. But if on a candid self-examination we find that we do not believe it, then the whole Prayer Book crumples; and there is no longer any question of mere revision: what we need is virtually a new Wordsworthian prayer book.

It is, however, very difficult to take seriously a document which is nearly 300 years old in its latest passages and 400 in the main. The physical universe it contemplates is not merely pre-Einsteinian but pre-Newtonian, not merely pre-Newtonian, but pre-Copernican. Creative evolution has no place in it; and this means that the Book of Common Prayer has no place in modern religious thought. Frankly, the book is worn out. It is past repair. And if and when a new one is established by Act of Parliament a clause should be added making revision compulsory every six years at most. I have said elsewhere that the law of change is the law of God; and Churches which deny this and try to keep their hold on the people by rituals stereotyped for eternity will presently find their already quarter-filled temples quite empty.

[192 ?]

147

On Ritual, Religion, and the Intolerableness of Tolerance

The original title of this essay was 'The Church Versus Religion', and its topic, we would say today, is œcumenicity. The framework, of course, has changed, since Shaw is thinking in terms of a suitable religion for the British Empire, but the problem itself is very much alive and has been taken up even in the Councils of Rome. Shaw poses here the paradoxical religious needs of mankind: to be united in a common brotherhood and at the same time to recognize in every human being a Separate Church.

In ranging from high ritualism to Quakerism and the Christian Science of Mary Baker Eddy, Shaw mentions the forgotten Émile Coué (1857–1926), the French psychologist, whose self-induced optimism reached the proportions of a fad in the post-War years, when people were advised to keep repeating to themselves, 'Every day in every way I'm getting better and better!'

The essay is published here for the first time.

Such a caption as The Church Versus Religion begs the question whether the Churches are really opposed to religion. Proverbs like 'The nearer the Church, the further from God', or, 'Heaven for holiness: hell for company' are happy as witticisms; but no statesman could legislate on them, nor any Churchman apostatize on them, unless both had given up religion altogether as a bad job. Tolstoy, whose letters to certain churchmen have provoked the present discussion, did not shake the dust of the Greek Church off his feet because it was religious, nor even because, on its political side, it was violently and shockingly irreligious. On that ground he would have had to leave, not only the Greek Church, but the world. Churches can repent and can reform; can purify their hearts and ennoble their rituals; can defy ambitious and tyrannical princes and either make them come to Canossa or suffer the worst they can inflict; can, in short, raise themselves from 'harmful sects', as Tolstoy rightly called the Church he left, to mighty spiritual powers, without committing suicide and abandoning their flocks to the world, the flesh, and the devil.

Tolstoy's real reason for leaving the Church was that he had no personal use for it. Its ritual, which helped others to a religious mood, only exasperated him, much as Jackson's Te Deum might have exasperated Beethoven. The preacher who seemed to the moujik and the little shopkeeper a wise and holy man must have often seemed to Tolstoy a noodle making an absurd mess of his job.

But even if the music had been by Beethoven, and the preacher another Peter or even another Christ, Tolstoy would have appreciated them only as a connoisseur appreciates a masterpiece of art. He would not have needed them for the making of his soul. That was his own business, which he could do so well for himself that a ritual and a priest could only distract him. For this reason he was an anti-Ritualist, and in England or America would have been a Quaker if he could have endured even a Quakers' meeting.

He need not have gone far to find men no less religious than himself to whom the forms in which he apprehended his religion seemed as idolatrous as the ikons of the Greek Church seemed to him. 'I believe', said Tolstoy, 'in God the Father, who sent me into this world so that I should fulfil His law'. A Bergsonian evolutionist would have replied, 'This conception of a Father is the superstition of a cottager. The *élan vital* in which I believe cannot be represented by anything so corporeal, though as I, too, believe that it sent me into the world to do its will, I am as religious a man as you'.

Beside the Bergsonians he might have found many people at the opposite extreme of intellectual development, to whom even so familiar a concept as a Father is no use unless he is seen and felt as well as conceived. They can pray to some material object only, were it only a stone that overhangs them threateningly or has something uncanny about its shape.

All the religious conflicts and bigotries and persecutions and wars of religion and *autos da fé* and so forth are misunderstandings between the men who apprehend God directly and intimately in the abstract (say Platonically), and those who can reach him only through symbols and ceremonies.

Let me state the case in due order from the beginning, using for convenience sake, the term Quaker (it is more homelike than Platonist) to denote the man at one end of the scale, and the term Ritualist to denote the man at the other.

There has always been, and always will be, a division between the Ritualist and the Quaker. There is no reason for quarrelling over it. There is room in the world for George Fox and the Pope. The trouble begins only when an attempt is made to force ritual on Fox, or to smash the statues and extinguish the candles in the Pope's chapel. Religion takes different men in different ways; and if they would accept that fact instead of trying to force their ways on one another, a process which involves the utter extinction of the religious spirit the moment it is even contemplated, both the Ritualist and the Quaker would be free to develop their states of grace to the utmost.

The first thing to grasp is that ritual is not religion, nor the absence of ritual irreligion. One man will not enter a church on any persuasion: he will not even call it a church: he calls it a steeplehouse. Another man haunts churches because he finds that in them he can meditate or pray better than anywhere else; but he flies from them the moment he is interrupted by the entry of the priest and the choristers in procession. Yet another man goes to church for the service alone: he never dreams of entering a church at any other time; and until the ritual begins he will busy himself disposing of his hat and umbrella, and noting that old Jones must be still down with lumbago as he has not come to church, and that young Smith has bought a new coat at last. But at the first word of the service he will buckle-to and be as pious as he can. Far from feeling that the priest and the service are coming between him and his God, and resenting them as a distracting intrusion, he clings to them because they are doing for him something that he cannot do for himself. The fact that the priest is there, and is not dressed as men of the world are dressed, and does not speak as they do, makes him feel that God must be there in the background, just as the sight of a liveried butler on the doorstep of a great man, and of the sentries at the palace gates, convinces him that the great man exists, and that the king is a reality. For what more convincing proof of a nearness of God can there be than the bodily vision of His house and of His servants?

Now it is very hard for these three different men to believe in one another's religiousness. To Number Three

Number One must be an atheist, because he not only does not go to church, but denies its sacredness. Number Two, who prowls about churches when there is no service going on, and leaves them when the congregation arrives, is clearly either a lunatic or a thief watching for an opportunity to break open the money-boxes or steal the Communion plate. Number One and Number Two regard Number Three as a Pharisee and a hypocrite. Number One suspects Number Two, who prays in the steeplehouse, of being half ritualist, half dilettant. When they go to extremes, Number One becomes an iconoclast, smashing everything in the cathedrals that he can reach, and insulting and murdering priests; and Number Three makes laws that Number One shall come to church whether he likes it or not, on pain of pillory, mutilation, outlawry, or the stake. Number Two is never powerful enough to go to extremes. If he were, he would keep Number Three and his priests out of the church, and keep Number One in the county jail.

When this sort of thing begins, there is an end of religion. Number Three, who, being usually in the majority, has most power of social and political coercion, attacks not only the man who does not go to church, but the man who goes to church at which the service differs in the slightest detail from that at his own church. In Ulster, men who go to the Protestant church throw bombs into groups of little children because the parents of those children go to the Roman Catholic church. They do so as champions of God, to the great amusement of the devil. They are provoked to this by the records of the Holy Office, or Inquisition, the proceedings of which moved the humane and genuinely religious Voltaire, who himself erected a church to God, to exclaim, as he contemplated the established Church of his country, *Écrasez l'infâme!* Whereupon Number Three concluded

that Voltaire must be an atheist, and believed that he died
in horrible terror and remorse, not because this was true,
but because Number Three liked to believe that an atheist
died that way, even when he also believed that God had
warned him that there are no bands in death for the wicked;
that their strength is firm; that they are not troubled as
other men.

Number One cannot mistake Number Three for an
atheist. He mistakes him for something much more revolting
than an atheist: an idolator. An Ulster Protestant, when he
sees a Papist (as he calls him) lighting a candle before a
statue of the Blessed Virgin, feels exactly as Robinson
Crusoe did when he burnt the tribal idol, or as Moses did
when he found his people worshipping the golden calf.
Mahomet in his reaction against idolatry stamped on Islam
a law that makes it impossible today to place any image of
man or beast in a mosque. Machiavelli, an ultra-Ulsterman,
though he was never in Ulster, hated priests with a mortal
hatred, and might logically have adopted the creed of
Mahomet, who excluded priests from his system as religiously as images. In vain does the Laodicean man of the
world, the Gallio,[1] or the impatiently Protestant Jonathan
Swift, ask what these people are quarrelling about? what it
matters whether a man prays and preaches in a black gown
or a white vestment? whether he raises a winecup above his
head before drinking or not? whether the wafer is regarded
as bread eaten in memory of the bread that Christ broke at
his last supper or as the body of God? Men who understand
the issues behind the symbolism are not indifferent: their
intense abhorrence of idolatry on the one hand, and of
atheism on the other, is at stake on every one of these details;
and they will slaughter and lay waste, burn women alive,
beat children savagely, sink and demolish, act so as to make

[1] See Acts 18: 12–17

153

the tiger and the serpent, the lightning and the earthquake, seem beneficent in comparison; and all this with the name of God not only on their lips, but in their hearts.

When we have the two extremes of a case clearly in mind, we have no difficulty in understanding the position of the persons who are somewhere on the scale between them. These are the great majority; for there are relatively few out-and-outers in religion. Anyone who has been in a mosque can testify that though there is nominally no priest there, the Imaums who lead the prayers and conduct the ceremonies fill, in the imagination of the worshippers of Allah, the place of the clergy and priests in the Christian churches, and that a Moorish Marabout has all the powers and all the sanctity of a medieval Christian bishop. True, there are no graven images or likenesses of anything that is in heaven above or in the earth beneath or in the water under the earth; but the elaborate decoration, the symbols and texts, the majestic architecture that is made homelike for Allah by the carpeted floor, are capable of influencing the mind of the spectators quite as powerfully as the imagery in Christian cathedrals.

The mass of mankind must have something to worship that the senses can apprehend. The Church of England began with a resolute effort to repudiate the anthropomorphic conception of God: its first article of belief is that God is a spirit without body, parts, or passions. Yet if it were to exclude from its communion today the people to whom God is the figure we see in Raphael's Vision of Ezekiel, and in Blake's illustrations to the Book of Job, it would be a negligible sect instead of a national Church. The four articles numbered 28 to 31 were a desperate attempt to make room in the same Church for Puritans who, though they lived too soon to read Sir James Frazer's Golden Bough, yet identified the Mass with the heathen Mexican ceremony

154

of eating the god, and for Catholics who believed literally in transubstantiation. There are High churches to please the Anglican Catholics and Low churches to please the Protestants. Those who cannot stomach prelacy will not join an Episcopalian Church; but they can become Presbyterians. The last straw that breaks the churchgoer's back is often a very light one. A single candle on the Communion table, or a right or left turn of the celebrant reading the service, may drive one worshipper away to a church where there is neither candle on the table nor pivot in the parson, and attract another to it.

The persecuting spirit acts in opposite directions. At first it meant an attempt to force heretics into churches. Charlemagne offered his heathen prisoners of war the choice between baptism and death. Queen Elizabeth told the Catholics and Puritans that she had done her best to make a Church that would satisfy both of them, and that they must come to it every Sunday or go to prison. As she overlooked the fact that there was a third alternative, America, Puritan Massachusetts and Catholic Maryland were among the consequences; but the point is that she wanted to compel people to come to her Church, not to repel them from its doors. Yet the inevitable result of treating as enemies the people who will not come to your Church is that you end by refusing to let them come even when they want to. Mahomet summoned the whole world to Mecca; but when Captain Burton went there in 1853 he did so at the risk of his life, carefully disguised as a Mussulman. I have seen an Englishman in Tangiers dragged violently away from the door of a mosque into which he was peeping. Thus the heretic is so hated that he is denied his right to conversion and salvation: he is killed because he will not worship in the temple, and killed equally if he attempts to enter it.

The evils of intolerance are so monstrous and so well

advertised that the Laodicean Centre, as we may call the easy-going majority, have set up Toleration as a virtue, and established it in law to some extent. But their success is only apparent. What is called Toleration is only submission to the fact that after many bloody trials Catholics and Protestants, Churchmen and Dissenters, Hindus and Mahometans, Buddhists and Shintos, have found that they cannot exterminate one another, and must agree to live and let live until luck gives one of them a decisive upper hand. The Laodiceans have never been able to prevent the religious people from dragging them sooner or later into wars of religion; and civilization does nothing to diminish the ferocity of these wars. The British Empire is specially hampered by the number and variety of its fanaticisms. White Christians are only about 11 per cent of the population. In India alone 33 native languages are more spoken than English. In addition to the 17-or-so varieties of Christians which the United States have to handle, the British Empire has to drive in single harness hundreds of millions of Hindus, Sikhs, Jains, Buddhists, Parsees, and Mahometans, to say nothing of divisions that the compilers of western books of reference have been unable to classify. The Jew is everywhere; and the attempt to shepherd him into a definitely localized Zion in Palestine has only brought his faith into a definitely localized conflict with the Islam of its native Arabs. It is natural for the American to preach Toleration to all these fanatics, because his very existence is due to a flight of persecuted but utterly intolerant men from intolerance; but his sermons are wasted breath. We must face the fact that no man will tolerate what he believes to be a false and mischievous religion whilst he has the means of persecuting and suppressing it.

Let the American who, fancying himself tolerant, is surprised by this statement, consider a little. If he were ruling India, would he tolerate Suttee and the car of Juggernaut? Would he tolerate Thuggee, the worship of Kali, goddess of blood, who demands from her devotees, not prayers and good works, but murders? Does he tolerate Voodoo? These questions answer themselves in the negative: nobody but a lunatic dreams of toleration for such beliefs in practice.

Bring it nearer home. If he is a materialist atheist, would he tolerate the Plymouth Brethren if he could help it? If he is a Plymouth Brother, would he tolerate atheism if he could help it? Is he quite sound on the Jewish question? Even if he is a Laodicean, and is prepared to tolerate all religions and irreligions for the sake of a quiet life, is that a reason for tolerating Ulster Calvinism and Ultramontanism? I cannot exhaust all the particular cases which raise the question of toleration; but I do not believe there is a man or woman on earth who cannot be fitted with a case in the which he or she is an uncompromising advocate of ruthless persecution. To be convinced of this it is only necessary to turn from the adults to the children. Granted that your neighbour must be left undisturbed in his belief that he may be predestined to spend eternity in boiling brimstone, driving himself half mad by continually thinking about it, is he to be allowed to lay his children's souls waste by urging that doctrine on them before they are old enough to dare go upstairs by themselves in the dark? If Shelley's children were taken away from him because he held that the god of Calvinistic Predestination is a fable, and if he were not, would be a fiend, are the people who agree with Shelley now that he is accepted as a prophet and a saint, likely to allow Calvinism to be taught to infants as divine truth in the public elementary schools for which they have to pay?

No. Toleration as an expediency may be very advisable;

157

but as a principle it is out of the question. Persecution may
be so inexpedient in many cases that no sane person would
insist on it; but when expediency is on the side of persecution, as, for example, on the Prohibition issue, everyone can
see that there is not the smallest difference in principle
between persecuting a toper and persecuting a Thug. In
prejudice, of course, there is all the difference in the world.
Speaking as a man of prejudice I should say that when you
prevent me from doing anything I want to do, that is persecution; but when I prevent you from doing anything you
want to do, that is law, order, and morals. After 1917 in
America there was a savage persecution of Bolshevism.
Several of its victims are still in prison. Do you, respectable
Yankee, call that persecution? Are you going to have those
victims released? Of course not. You believe in Toleration;
but you draw the line at Bolshevism. I blame you for this;
but I am not blaming your intolerance: I am blaming your
ignorance. If you believe that Bolshevism means theft,
murder, communism in women, and everything horrid
(your English great-grandfather believed the same things
about Jacobinism, and talked about Washington as you do
about Lenin) why, then you are right to persecute Bolshevism. But you are not right to believe such manifest guff and
bugaboo.

Is there then no remedy for the evils brought on us by
our bigotry? None, in my opinion, except a hair of the dog
that bit us. What we need is more religion to get us to the
root of the matter. There is a science of religion in which
we should all be instructed. When Mrs Eddy set up the
Church of Christ Scientist, she was very well inspired indeed. Christ was not tolerant: he was not prepared to
tolerate money-changers and traders in sacrificial beasts in
the Temple. He warned the Pharisees that there were
blasphemies that are unpardonable, and denounced them

as vipers: that is, creatures whom the most tolerant cannot tolerate. But he refused altogether to make any distinction on the point of eligibility for salvation between Jew and Gentile, baptized and circumcized. He not only refrained from proselytizing, but expressly warned the proselytizers that a man's religious consciousness is like a fertile field, so that if they tried to root up the tares in it they would root up the wheat as well and leave him without any religion at all. It never occurred to him to ask a Jew to cease being a Jew: he simply exhorted him to become a Christian as well as a Jew. Christianity as Christ preached it is applicable to all the Churches and religions that are consistent with human society. A Thug cannot be a Christian; but a Mahometan can: a Buddhist can: a Parsee can: a Jain can; and though there are greater difficulties in the case of the varieties of pseudo-Christians now overrunning the world outside Asia, there is hope even for them.

When men are united in a common religion, there will be no persecution problem. What we have to deal with now is the fact that they cannot be so united until the common religion presents itself to them in many different forms. If you ask me why not, I reply that all men's minds have not the same scope. The form of worship that brings one man into communion with God may move another to impatient derision as a childish mummery or even as a blasphemy. God without body, parts or passions, though legally the God of the Church of England, is no god at all to the man who can apprehend no moral force that is not anthropomorphic. Rousseau told us that if we would only get rid of our miracle stories the whole world would fall at the feet of Christ; but he was wrong: there are multitudes of simple people – Italian peasants for example – who cannot be induced to worship any saint or Saviour who does not prove his title to their veneration by performing miracles; so that their Church has actually to provide sham miracles to save their souls. The popular fiction of hell is a very horrible one: so much so that if it were not tacitly dropped in cultured urban congregations, the Churches would die of it; but Mahomet, though personally humane to a degree that makes his personal career somewhat scandalous to Western tastes, was forced to elaborate the story of the brimstone lake by the most ingeniously disgusting inventions, knowing that men who are morbidly attracted by tragically terrible punishments, will recoil from the ridicule that attends squalor, dirt, stench, and infirmity. And what drove him to this was that he had to govern men of whom many were quite incapable of conceiving divine displeasure unless it had what modern diplomatists call sanctions: that is, unless it was visited on those who incurred it in extremely unpleasant ways.

These are only the more obvious cases of the rule that no two men can have exactly the same faith unless they have exactly the same mental capacity. St Thomas Aquinas was an Italian Catholic; and the peasants of the Abruzzi were Italian Catholics; but as St Thomas was a very subtle schoolman, and the peasants were very superstitious fieldmen, they understood Catholicism quite differently, and had not in fact the same religion at all; whilst the avowed differences between the Italian peasant and the Tibetan peasant, between St Thomas and Plato or Aristotle, were no deeper than differences of dialect.

To take a less extreme contrast, there are men of wide culture and reading, and of considerable achievement in physical science, who are so matter-of-fact in their mental constitution that they can see nothing in the Athanasian Creed but an arithmetical impossibility. They say that if there is one god there is one god, and if there are three gods there are three gods, but there cannot be one and three at the same time. But the three in one and the one in three presented no difficulty to Athanasius: it seemed so simple to him that he went the length of declaring that anyone with so little intellect as to boggle at it would be damned. To many of us the notion of a man being damned for purely intellectual inadequacy is revolting: we feel that everything will be forgiven to him whose heart is in the right place, and that Athanasius himself deserved to be damned for his uncharitableness, in spite of his having written the most intellectually subtle page in the Prayer Book of the Church of England; but there is a great deal to be said for a sharp reminder to us that good intentions are no excuse for stupidity, and that if people are to be damned at all, it had better be the fools than the rascals.

If we try to group all these differences, and scores of others which it would be wearisome to state, so as to arrive at some generalization by which our mind can deal compendiously with them, we will find that, as to worship, they arrange themselves along the scale at one end of which is the Quaker and at the other the Ritualist, and, as to belief, along the scale from the abstract to the concrete. At one end of this scale of belief is a Creative Spirit, a Force of Nature, as immaterial until incarnated in its living works as a part without an actor; and at the other the visible corporal humanly-emotional figure depicted by Blake and Raphael, or fashioned with a hundred hands and an elephant's trunk by Hindoo artificers, or as a man with a hawk's head by the Egyptians, until you come to the mere block of stone on which the human imagination fastens as sacred in the stage in which it must have something concrete to cling to to save it from madness.

In the understanding and recognition of this inequality of apprehension between men lies the secret of tolerance. Take my own case. When my affairs do not oblige me to be in

London, I live in a little village of 130 scattered inhabitants. It has a church and a Rector. My own house was for a long time the Rectory; and my tenancy of it endowed the church. When the churchwardens apply to me at the usual seasons I contribute; and when the hat goes round for special expenses for repairs to the building, I pay my share of what may be necessary to keep it standing. I am on intimate terms with the Rector. I am, in short, a local pillar of the Church; and I visit it occasionally. But I have never attended a service there. Whether from defect or excess of intellect, I cannot use the Church of England ritual either as spiritual food or to express and demonstrate my religion. The last time I tried it was when my mother died. She was not a Church of England ritualist; but she had no prejudices nor bigotries; and she would have agreed with me that when there was a chaplain attached to the crematorium, it would have been a little shabby to save his fee and consign her body to the fire without any ceremony at all. And so the Church of England burial service was read. But I found it morbid and heathenish. It was all wrong for my mother and all wrong for me. Later on, my sister followed my mother; and she left a will in which she expressly barred any ritual. But here I found myself up against a religious need. When I found myself in the chapel of the crematorium surrounded by her friends, many of them suffering from a distress that needed some recognition and expression, I found that it was not possible to order the officials to dispose of the remains that still had my sister's shape as if they were a scuttleful of coals. I had to improvise a ceremony which was none the less a funeral ceremony because it consisted of an address by myself in my own words. This was possible for me: I am a practised public speaker, and by profession an author. But of the relatives of those who die not one in a thousand could compose a suitable address, or dare utter it in public if he or she could. For the vast majority there must be a form of words provided and a professional speaker to utter them impressively. To bury without a word or gesture would be to them to bury 'like a dog'. How then could I possibly live in a village and refuse my share in the provision of a ceremony to my neighbours merely because the ceremony did not fit my own case, and I was able to supply one for myself? It would be the act not merely of a bigot, but of a curmudgeon.

Later still a friend of mine induced me to go to the nuptially famous London church of St George's, Hanover Square, to see him married. Here my feelings were quite decisive. I felt that I would live and die celibate rather than take part in such a ceremony and thereby seem to assent to its unwholesome and nonsensical comparison of my mating to the mystical union of Christ with the Church, and to that very disingenuous reference to St Paul by which the authors of the Prayer Book tried to make the best of what they evidently considered (as he did) a rather questionable business. I congratulated myself on having had the alternative of civil marriage open to me. But in the view of strict Catholics, Anglican or Roman, I am not married at all. Only, they need not go on to say that I am living in sin; for on my part the sin would lie in giving a false expression to my religious feeling. But what is false for me may be true for another; and I have not the smallest objection to its being provided for him out of the common funds to which I contribute. He has to contribute to the common fund out of which the civil registrar who marries me is paid; and if this reciprocal fiscal toleration works smoothly I do not see why reciprocal spiritual toleration should be impossible.

If I were asked to fill up an ordinary official form containing a column for my religion I should probably save the officials trouble by writing The Episcopal Church of Ireland, of which I am a member by baptism. But if I were asked to describe myself for the purposes of a serious investigation of the religious condition of the country, I should call myself a Creative Evolutionist for reasons which I have already sufficiently explained in my Preface to Back to Methuselah; but I might quite fairly write myself down a Platonist or amateur Quaker, using the word amateur to imply that I am not an enlisted member of the Society of Friends, in which, by the way, genuine Quakers are hardly commoner than they are elsewhere, because, as membership of the Society is largely hereditary, and genuine Quakerism is a gift of God, I suspect that in most Quaker meetings, if the Spirit moved a young man to get up and say anything unexpected, or indeed to say anything at all, there would be as much scandalized indignation as if he had 'brawled' in a cathedral. In essentials I am Protestant and Quaker, because the intervention of any priest between me and my God would be to me the most unbearable of impertinences, and because I need no visible image, no temple made with hands, no acted fable, to enable me to apprehend as much of my relation to the universe as is humanly apprehensible. Nor do I use or need forms of prayer. When I was a child, and said my prayers at night as I had been taught to do, I composed my own prayers, ending up with the Lord's Prayer: rather, I think, as a gesture of politeness to its author, than as a prayer. Thus, even in my nonage, I was independent of the set forms of heavenly communion; and my religion, for what it is worth, needs no ceremonial aid from writer, builder, musical composer, priest, or Church, though nobody has been more nourished by their works than I. Nothing must come between me and the spirit that moves within me; and though I do not walk by the inner light alone, but by all the light I can get, from without or within, yet I must interpret what I see for myself. And if that is not the quintessence of Quakerism, and indeed of genuine Quakerism, I do not know what Quakerism means.

But what could be more unreasonable and cruel than for me to try to deprive my ritualist neighbours of their set prayers, their praises, their legends, their temples and masses, their anthems, their coloured windows, their pictures and statues, and their hierarchies of vestured priests, especially as all these give extraordinary delight to my sense of art when their poets and painters and sculptors and orators have been religiously inspired, and often awaken my religious sense as sun and rain awaken seed? It would be no less unreasonable and cruel on their part to force their ritual on me and persecute me because another fashion of religion is natural to me.

The mischief of persecution lies, not in our different ways, but in the unfounded inferences we draw from them. A friend of mine, since dead, an army officer with the education and knowledge and experience of the world implied by that position, once said to me, 'Well, Shaw, I don't know what you think about religion; but I know for a fact that the son of the Vicar up at ——— is the father of the house-maid's illegitimate child; and you may tell me that the Bible is true after that if you like; but I shan't believe you.' To this man the whole validity of his religion, and indeed of all religion, depended on the success of one of its ministers in imposing conventional chastity on his son. We cannot laugh at him because we all know that such grotesque tests of religion are too common to be a laughing matter. Immense numbers of people would conclude unhesitatingly that because I do not attend Church services I can have no religion and therefore no conscience. Of these numbers many believe that if a man prays to the Blessed Virgin to intercede for him with God, he is an idolator who, if he had the power, would consign thousands of his fellow citizens to the rack and stake. To such sophisticated souls it is not enough to believe in God: you must call him God and nothing else: if you call him Allah or Vishnu or (of late years) even Gott, you are a heathen.

The difficulty is an old one. Everybody is sincerely in favour of religion, of duty, of goodness and justice, of all things that are lovely and of good report; but it is not enough to be in favour of these things: you must be able to recognize them when you meet them. Annas and Caiaphas had a remarkable opportunity in that way; but they missed is because they mistook a man more religious than themselves, though in a different fashion, for a blasphemer and a scoundrel.

Nowadays intolerance is rife between sects so anti-clerical that the mere suggestion of their possibility would have made Caiaphas tear himself beardless and naked. Take for example the formulas of the Church of Christ Scientist as prescribed by Mrs Eddy. Mrs Eddy, as it is now appearing, was much sounder in her science than the medical profession in her day, with its materialistic view of the living body as a purely mechanical and chemical phenomenon; yet she is denounced and reviled not only by the materialistic doctors and surgeons, but by the disciples of M. Coué, who makes invalids cure themselves by the formula 'I am getting better and better every minute'. The cures of Christian Science are obviously fundamentally identical with the cures of M. Coué; but Mrs Eddy's formula will not start the self-healing process in Smith, who is subsequently cured triumphantly by M. Coué; and Jones, who has told himself in vain for weeks that he is getting better from hour to hour, is no sooner taken in hand by one of Mrs Eddy's ministers than he makes a perfect recovery. The plan of St James, as practised by the Peculiar People, succeeds where both Mrs Eddy and M. Coué's plan fail. Even a doctor's prescription

166

has been known to succeed with people who have faith in it, and would succeed much oftener if doctors did not persist in poisoning the chalice by putting drugs into it. None of these plans cure me, because they have not found the exact sort of hocus-pocus that starts the miracle of healing and recreation in me; but I owe a great deal to the fact that having in my happily irreverent youth dismissed all the religions, and subsequently the scientific formulas as hocus-pocus, there was nothing to hinder me from going on to discover that all the hocus-pocuses are equally good for the people whose capacities and idiosyncrasies they hit off. Thus they are at once all wrong and all right; and he who calls his brother a fool for clinging to one of them is a fool himself. The texts to hang out like banners to confound bigots are (from Tennyson) 'God fulfils himself in many ways', and (my favourite Scripture) 'What doth the Lord require of thee but to do justly, and to love mercy, and to walk humbly before thy God?'

Though the moral of all this is that you must suffer your neighbour to serve God in his own way, however different it may be from yours, let no Church lazily conclude that its ritual needs no revision merely because it is sure to supply somebody's want. If the Church of England, for example, consoles itself for the loss of another hundred of the British intelligentsia by the accession of another million Polynesian and African converts from crude anthropophagy, her state will not be the more gracious. I take, after my manner, the extreme instance to make the position clear; but the danger lies in more insidious changes. If the Church is losing its hold on relatively clever and cultured people and filling their pews with relatively stupid and ignorant people, then, however slight the difference may be from year to year, it will tell perceptibly from lustrum to lustrum. The Dean of St Paul's, himself the greatest Platonist of us all, has said that if ordination be refused to all candidates who do not believe literally and unequivocally what they now have to profess to believe before they can be ordained, the ministry will presently consist exclusively of fools, bigots, and liars. This, which is so obviously true that the Church dares not rebuke the Dean for affirming it, however much it may wish he had said nothing, is not a wholesome state of things. And the Prayer Book has gone bad in the course of three centuries in other places than in the creeds and articles. The people they are good enough for are not good enough for a Church aiming at representing what is best in Christendom.

Then there is the quaint anarchy of the parsons by whose conduct most of their neighbours judge the Church. The Rector is the freeholder of his Rectory; and he may also be a rampant freethinker in politics and sociology. He claims and exercises all the liberties of a country gentleman, and wallows openly in class prejudices. Often he snubs the poor, and sides with the squire against them; he sees to it that servility and imperialist militarism are inculcated in the Church schools; he pitches the emblems of Christian peace into the cellar and waves the Union Jack the moment there is any question of war; he supports the way of the police as God's appointed way of dealing with crime; and he is equally free to preach the most extreme Bolshevist views in opposition to all this if his congregation will stand it. In the late war British clergymen who had to bury certain German soldiers who were killed in aeroplane raids actually altered the words of the burial service to express their personal refusal to admit that Englishmen and Germans, as the children of the Father of us all, are brothers; and though this was clearly either treachery to Christ or cowardice in the face of the mob: that is to say, a betrayal of duty for which a soldier would be shot, it was taken as a matter of course that a clergyman should behave like any irresponsible tramp

168

if he had a mind to. It was this sort of thing that made
Tolstoy so bitter against the Greek Church, and which
makes all the revolutionary movements anti-clerical, in spite
of the fact that Socialism, the main revolutionary movement of today, bases its policy on the conception of a truly
Catholic Church for the workers of all nations.

There is, in fact, no effective modern discipline in any of
the Churches. A Roman Catholic priest can be silenced;
but he is much more likely to be silenced for advocating the
wholesome practice of cremation, or declaring that animals
have quite soul enough to have rights as against cruel and
thoughtless men, than for making his Church ridiculous or
odious by insisting on such crudely literal acceptance of all
the Church's dogmas as must put them in the light of silly
superstitions before reasonably humane and well informed
people. As to a Church of England rector, he cannot be
silenced at all: his rectory is his castle; and he can be driven
from it only by general social pressure.

Up to a certain point this freedom of the individual priest
or minister, unless he is a hopeless crank, does more good
than harm. And beyond a certain point Churches will be
what their members, clerical and lay, make them, no matter
what their creeds, articles, and disciplines may be. But the
same may be said of any human organization; and yet an
organization that does not draw certain lines in faith and
conduct is not an organization at all, but a mob. The British
navy allows its admirals a latitude in writing to The Times
which can be explained only by its recognition of the fact
that no man can go through the ordeal of the quarter-deck
without becoming more or less crazy; but an admiral who
altered the Articles of War to suit his own political
prejudices, or who allowed rich officers to shirk their share
of the risks run by those who were the sons of parsons and
suchlike hard-ups (like Nelson), would be dismissed from

the service or certified as insane and sent to Copenhagen Hospital. You may be a very eccentric naval officer: you may swear like a fighting mate on an ocean tramp, and shake your fist in the king's face, and even flatly disobey orders if you can win a battle thereby; but you may not fight for the enemy when the battle is joined (however much you may sympathize with him), nor, in time of peace, may you, by example and precept, devote yourself to the sub-version of the principles of national defence and the encouragement of the slackers and shirkers as the most respectable persons in the ship. Consequently the navy has never fallen into contempt in England as the Church has, and as the courts have; and the explanation is that clergy-men are not effectively restrained from bringing religion, nor judges from bringing the law, into contempt. To the naval and military officer we do effectively and convincingly say, 'Be faithful to your profession, or get out.' To the officers of the Church and the Law, we say, 'Do what you please, and be damned.' With the result that it is we who are damned, unless we keep carefully out of the churches and out of the courts. And it is not possible for all of us to keep out of either.

The end of the discussion then is, for the present, that as some of the most religious men in the world have been mis-taken for atheists, like Voltaire, for mere gluttonous wine-bibbers, like Christ, for impostors, like Mahomet, and for superstitious humbugs, like many very honest nameless parsons and priests, we had better be careful how we judge one another, or put ourselves in the place of God by dictat-ing how our neighbour should serve Him. And also that any Church which makes a great fuss when a cathedral pillar sinks or a wall cracks, and collects a great sum to have the building under-pinned and made safe, but sees its creeds and services going crazy with age, and sinking and rifting and tumbling in all directions without saying a word about them except to swear that they are as safe as the Pyramids, and that those who are complaining that they will presently fall and bury the nation in their ruins are disreputable liars, that Church will end, as many churches have ended in England, in having buildings without congregations. Also, since people want up-to-date creeds and rituals, but care for nothing later than the fifteenth century in architecture (or, if they are connoisseurs, the twelfth), the carefully 'restored' churches will not attract even the better sort of sight-seeing tourists to fill the places of the worshippers their obsolete rituals have driven away.

[1922]

Preface to Saint Joan

Throughout his later years Shaw persistently claimed that he was a mystic. 'I exhausted rationalism when I got to the end of my second novel at the age of twenty-four,' he wrote his friend, Dame Laurentia McLachlan in 1924, 'and should have come to a dead stop if I had not proceeded to purely mystical assumptions.' Notwithstanding the brilliance of his dialectic, he claimed, with his most popular heroine, Saint Joan, that 'the voices come first and I find the reasons after'.

The nature of mystical phenomena cannot therefore be overlooked in any survey of Shaw's religious beliefs.

Joan's Voices and Visions

Joan's voices and visions have played many tricks with her reputation. They have been held to prove that she was mad, that she was a liar and impostor, that she was a sorceress (she was burned for this), and finally that she was a saint. They do not prove any of these things; but the variety of the conclusions reached shew how little our matter-of-fact historians know about other people's minds, or even about their own. There are people in the world whose imagination is so vivid that when they have an idea it comes to them as an audible voice, sometimes uttered by a visible figure.

Criminal lunatic asylums are occupied largely by murderers who have obeyed voices. Thus a woman may hear voices telling her that she must cut her husband's throat and strangle her child as they lie asleep; and she may feel obliged to do what she is told. By a medico-legal superstition it is held in our courts that criminals whose temptations present themselves under these illusions are not responsible for their actions, and must be treated as insane. But the seers of visions and the hearers of revelations are not always criminals. The inspirations and intuitions and unconsciously reasoned conclusions of genius sometimes assume similar illusions. Socrates, Luther, Swedenborg, Blake saw visions and heard voices just as Saint Francis and Saint Joan did. If Newton's imagination had been of the same vividly dramatic kind he might have seen the ghost of Pythagoras walk into the orchard and explain why the apples were falling. Such an illusion would have invalidated neither the theory of gravitation nor Newton's general sanity. What is more, the visionary method of making the discovery would not be a whit more miraculous than the normal method. The test of sanity is not the normality of the method but the reasonableness of the discovery. If Newton had been informed by Pythagoras that the moon was made of green cheese, then Newton would have been locked up. Gravitation, being a reasoned hypothesis which fitted remarkably well into the Copernican version of the observed physical facts of the universe, established Newton's reputation for extraordinary intelligence, and would have done so no matter how fantastically he had arrived at it. Yet his theory of gravitation is not so impressive a mental feat as his astounding chronology, which established him as the king of mental conjurors, but a Bedlamite king whose authority no one now accepts. On the subject of the eleventh horn of the beast seen by the prophet Daniel he was more fantastic than Joan, because his imagination was not dramatic but mathematical and therefore extraordinarily susceptible to numbers: indeed if all his works were lost except his chronology we should say that he was as mad as a hatter. As it is, who dares diagnose Newton as a madman?

In the same way Joan must be judged a sane woman in spite of her voices because they never gave her any advice that might not have come to her from her mother wit exactly as gravitation came to Newton. We can all see now, especially since the late war threw so many of our women into military life, that Joan's campaigning could not have been carried on in petticoats. This was not only because she did a man's work, but because it was morally necessary that sex should be left out of the question as between her and her comrades-in-arms. She gave this reason herself when she was pressed on the subject; and the fact that this entirely reasonable necessity came to her imagination first as an order from God delivered through the mouth of Saint Catherine does not prove that she was mad. The soundness of the order proves that she was unusually sane; but its form proves that her dramatic imagination played tricks with her senses. Her policy was also quite sound: nobody disputes that the relief of Orleans, followed up by the coronation at Rheims of the Dauphin as a counterblow to the suspicions then current of his legitimacy and consequently of his title, were military and political masterstrokes that saved France. They might have been planned by Napoleon or any other illusion proof genius. They came to Joan as an instruction from her Counsel, as she called her visionary saints; but she was none the less an able leader of men for imagining her ideas in this way.

The Evolutionary Appetite

What then is the modern view of Joan's voices and visions and messages from God? The nineteenth century said that they were delusions, but that as she was a pretty girl, and had been abominably ill-treated and finally done to death by a superstitious rabble of medieval priests hounded on by a corrupt political bishop, it must be assumed that she was the innocent dupe of these delusions. The twentieth century finds this explanation too vapidly commonplace, and demands something more mystic. I think the twentieth century is right, because an explanation which amounts to Joan being mentally defective instead of, as she obviously was, mentally excessive, will not wash. I cannot believe, nor, if I could, could I expect all my readers to believe, as Joan did, that three ocularly visible well dressed persons, named respectively Saint Catherine, Saint Margaret, and Saint Michael, came down from heaven and gave her certain instructions with which they were charged by God for her. Not that such a belief would be more improbable or fantastic than some modern beliefs which we all swallow; but there are fashions and family habits in belief, and it happens that, my fashion being Victorian and my family habit Protestant, I find myself unable to attach any such objective validity to the form of Joan's visions.

But that there are forces at work which use individuals for purposes far transcending the purpose of keeping these individuals alive and prosperous and respectable and safe and happy in the middle station in life, which is all any good bourgeois can reasonably require, is established by the fact that men will, in the pursuit of knowledge and of social readjustments for which they will not be a penny the better, and are indeed often many pence the worse, face poverty, infamy, exile, imprisonment, dreadful hardship, and death.

Even the selfish pursuit of personal power does not nerve men to the efforts and sacrifices which are eagerly made in pursuit of extensions of our power over nature, though these extensions may not touch the personal life of the seeker at any point. There is no more mystery about this appetite for knowledge and power than about the appetite for food: both are known as facts and as facts only, the difference between them being that the appetite for food is necessary to the life of the hungry man and is therefore a personal appetite, whereas the other is an appetite for evolution, and therefore a superpersonal need.

The diverse manners in which our imaginations dramatize the approach of the superpersonal forces is a problem for the psychologist, not for the historian. Only, the historian must understand that visionaries are neither impostors nor lunatics. It is one thing to say that the figure Joan recognized as St Catherine was not really St Catherine, but the dramatization by Joan's imagination of that pressure upon her of the driving force that is behind evolution which I have just called the evolutionary appetite. It is quite another to class her visions with the vision of two moons seen by a drunken person, or with Brocken spectres, echoes and the like. Saint Catherine's instructions were far too cogent for that; and the simplest French peasant who believes in apparitions of celestial personages to favoured mortals is nearer to the scientific truth about Joan than the Rationalist and Materialist historians and essayists who feel obliged to set down a girl who saw saints and heard them talking to her as either crazy or mendacious. If Joan was mad, all Christendom was mad too; for people who believe devoutly in the existence of celestial personages are every whit as mad in that sense as the people who think they see them. Luther, when he threw his inkhorn at the devil, was no more mad than any other Augustinian monk: he had a more vivid imagination, and had perhaps eaten and slept less: that was all.

The Mere Iconography does Not Matter

All the popular religions in the world are made apprehensible by an array of legendary personages, with an Almighty Father, and sometimes a mother and divine child, as the central figures. These are presented to the mind's eye in childhood; and the result is a hallucination which persists strongly throughout life when it has been well impressed. Thus all the thinking of the hallucinated adult about the fountain of inspiration which is continually flowing in the universe, or about the promptings of virtue and the revulsions of shame: in short, about aspiration and conscience, both of which forces are matters of fact more obvious than electro-magnetism, is thinking in terms of the celestial vision. And when in the case of exceptionally imaginative persons, especially those practising certain appropriate austerities, the hallucination extends from the mind's eye to the body's, the visionary sees Krishna or the Buddha or the Blessed Virgin or St Catherine as the case may be.

The Modern Education which Joan Escaped

It is important to everyone nowadays to understand this, because modern science is making short work of the hallucinations without regard to the vital importance of the things they symbolize. If Joan were reborn today she would be sent, first to a convent school in which she would be mildly taught to connect inspiration and conscience with St Catherine and St Michael exactly as she was in the fifteenth century, and then finished up with a very energetic training in the gospel of Saints Louis Pasteur and Paul Bert, who would tell her (possibly in visions but more probably in pamphlets) not to be a superstitious little fool, and to empty out St Catherine and the rest of the Catholic hagiology as an obsolete iconography of exploded myths. It would be rubbed into her that Galileo was a martyr, and his persecutors incorrigible ignoramuses, and that St Teresa's hormones had gone astray and left her incurably hyperpituitary or hyperadrenal or hysteroid or epileptoid or anything but asteroid. She would have been convinced by precept and experiment that baptism and receiving the body of her Lord were contemptible superstitions, and that vaccination and vivisection were enlightened practices. Behind her new Saints Louis and Paul there would be not only Science purifying Religion and being purified by it, but hypochondria, melancholia, cowardice, stupidity, cruelty, muckraking curiosity, knowledge without wisdom, and everything that the eternal soul in Nature loathes, instead of the virtues of which St Catherine was the figurehead. As to the new rites, which would be the saner Joan? the one who carried little children to be baptized of water and the spirit, or the one who sent the police to force their parents to have the most villainous racial poison we know thrust into their veins? the one who told them the story of the angel and Mary, or the one who questioned them as to their experiences of the Edipus complex? the one to whom the consecrated wafer was the very body of the virtue that was her salvation, or the one who looked forward to a precise and convenient regulation of her health and her desires by a nicely calculated diet of thyroid extract, adrenalin, thymin, pituitrin, and insulin, with pick-me-ups of hormone stimulants, the blood being first carefully fortified with antibodies against all possible infections by inoculations of infected bacteria and serum from infected animals, and against old age by surgical extirpation of the reproductive ducts or weekly doses of monkey gland?

It is true that behind all these quackeries there is a certain body of genuine scientific physiology. But was there any the less a certain body of genuine psychology behind St Catherine and the Holy Ghost? And which is the healthier mind? the saintly mind or the monkey gland mind? Does not the present cry of Back to the Middle Ages, which has been incubating ever since the pre-Raphaelite movement began, mean that it is no longer our Academy pictures that are intolerable, but our credulities that have not the excuse of being superstitions, our cruelties that have not the excuse of barbarism, our persecutions that have not the excuse of religious faith, our shameless substitution of successful swindlers and scoundrels and quacks for saints as objects of worship, and our deafness and blindness to the calls and visions of the inexorable power that made us, and will destroy us if we disregard it? To Joan and her contemporaries we should appear as a drove of Gadarene swine, possessed by all the unclean spirits cast out by the faith and civilization of the Middle Ages, running violently down a steep place into a hell of high explosives. For us to set up our condition as a standard of sanity, and declare Joan mad because she never condescended to it, is to prove that we are not only lost but irredeemable. Let us then once for all drop all nonsense about Joan being cracked, and accept her as at least as sane as Florence Nightingale, who also combined a very simple iconography of religious belief with a mind so exceptionally powerful that it kept her in continual trouble with the medical and military panjandrums of her time.

Failures of the Voices

That the voices and visions were illusory, and their wisdom all Joan's own, is shewn by the occasions on which they failed her, notably during her trial, when they assured her that she would be rescued. Here her hopes flattered her; but they were not unreasonable: her military colleague La Hire was in command of a considerable force not so very far off; and if the Armagnacs, as her party was called, had really wanted to rescue her, and had put anything like her own vigour into the enterprise, they could have attempted it with very fair chances of success. She did not understand that they were glad to be rid of her, nor that the rescue of a prisoner from the hands of the Church was a much more serious business for a medieval captain, or even a medieval king, than its mere physical difficulty as a military exploit suggested. According to her lights her expectation of a rescue was reasonable; therefore she heard Madame Saint Catherine assuring her it would happen, that being her way of finding out and making up her own mind. When it became evident that she had miscalculated: when she was led to the stake, and La Hire was not thundering at the gates of Rouen nor charging Warwick's men at arms, she threw over Saint Catherine at once, and recanted. Nothing could be more sane or practical. It was not until she discovered that she had gained nothing by her recantation but close imprisonment for life that she withdrew it, and deliberately and explicitly chose burning instead: a decision which shewed not only the extraordinary decision of her character, but also a Rationalism carried to its ultimate human test of suicide. Yet even in this the illusion persisted; and she announced her relapse as dictated to her by her voices.

[1924]

Personal Immortality

This was Shaw's contribution to a newspaper discussion of 'Where Are the Dead?' It appeared in the *Daily News* of 6 June 1928.

I am butting into this controversy, not with any intention of settling it, but merely to suggest a variation of its method. I have noticed that the point under discussion is stated as whether 'we' are immortal, whether 'the dead' survive, or whether 'the soul' perishes with the body.

The style is the leading article style, the royal style, or the style of Italian and Highland politeness, in which the individual is not you but she, the she denoting an abstraction of honour and excellency, as to which anything is credible and arguable.

This gives immense scope to the discussion and elasticity to its terms; but it takes our feet off the earth so completely as to enable the controversialists to prove that there may be such a thing as immortality without producing the faintest conviction that any particular Tom, Dick or Harry, Susan, Sophronia or Jane ever was or will be immortal.

What I propose is that your next few contributors shall discuss, not whether 'we' are immortal, or whether the soul is immortal, or whether the dead are still seeking lodgings in infinite space, but whether I, Bernard Shaw, am going to persist to all eternity in a universe utterly unable to get rid of me, no matter how desperately tired it may become of the Shavianismus, or how intolerably bored I may be by myself. Can there never be enough of me? Never too much of me?

Also, am I myself to have any say in the matter? Am I or am I not to be allowed to hand myself back to my creator, and say 'Will you be so kind as to pulp this worn out article, and remanufacture it, if possible, without any of the glaring defects which have made it so troublesome to myself and others?'

For the guidance of those who will undertake this discussion, I had better say that as far as I know no person has ever doubted that I did not exist before October 1855. Now the arguments that prove that I cannot have an end seem to me to prove equally that I cannot have had a beginning. Many persons think that it would have been better if I could not have had a beginning. But I most certainly had a beginning. The event can be precisely dated.

I may be a brick made from the eternal clay; in fact, people to whom I have injudiciously lent money have sometimes called me a brick; but the brick, though made of the clay, is not the clay.

Nobody but a lunatic would maintain that a brick existed before it was baked, or will still be a brick when it has crumbled into dust. Consequently, all the arguments that prove that my non-existence is impossible must be ruled out.

As a matter of fact, I have non-existed; and the discussion must address itself to proving or disproving that the non-existence that was possible before 1855 can never be possible again.

With this hint I leave your contributors to their stupendous theme: an eternity of G.B.S. Imagine it, if you can! Millions upon millions of Shaw plays! Billions upon billions of letters to the Press, intensely irritating to many worthy citizens! To be 'a fellow of infinite jest', not, like poor Yorick, figuratively, but literally!

Chesterton, too. He also will be bombinating for ever and ever, world without end. And Wells and Belloc in sempiternal controversy! How if we became really convinced of it – not on paper, where anybody can be convinced of anything, but genuinely in the centre of our life – and immediately went off our chumps, as I for one most certainly should?

Frederick the Great was very far from being in all respects a trustworthy spiritual guide; but when he said to the soldier who was running away, 'Confound you, do you want to live for ever?' he said a mouthful.

One word more. Let no controversialist try to evade the point by assuring me that I shall survive, not as myself, but as the just man made perfect. He might as well tell me that the chariot of Pharaoh survives in the Rolls Royce.

When I use the word 'I' (as I frequently do) I mean myself, with all my imperfections (if any) on my head, and my eyebrows turning up, and not down like those of my friend Mr George Robey. I mean the celebrated G.B.S., almost unbearably individualized, with his consciousness and his memories, his tricks and his manners, complete and exact in his G.B. Essence.

Otherwise the controversy is about nothing.

[1928]

A New Stanza for the National Anthem

Sharing with Sir Edward Elgar the distaste for a National Anthem which presumed to instruct the Almighty to dispose of England's enemies by confounding their knavish tricks, Shaw, at one time, suggested an alternative stanza.

(A variant for 'God Save the Queen' altered the fifth verse to read, 'Let her God's handmaid be.')

O Lord our God arise!
All our salvation lies
In Thy great hands.
Centre his thoughts on Thee,
Let him God's captain be,
Thine to eternity,
God save the King.

The Adventures of the Black Girl in Her Search for God

In South Africa in 1932, Shaw, driving an unfamiliar vehicle, lost control of it and smashed into the rough veldt, causing his wife serious injury. Restlessly awaiting Charlotte's recovery, he set himself to writing a religious saga structured like Voltaire's *Candide*.

The Adventures of the Black Girl in Her Search for God follows the path of a simple but highly curious native who has been told by the missionaries, 'Seek and ye shall find'. She quickly finds (and destroys with her knob-kerry) the savage gods of Moses and of Job, and pauses not much longer for the despairing Ecclesiastes or the howling prophet, Micah.

The African forest in which she searches is not entirely chronological, and in flight from the prophet she comes upon a more modern god – Science – in the obvious guise of Ivan Pavlov.

'What am I running away from?' she said to herself, pulling herself up. 'I'm not afraid of that dear noisy old man.'

'Your fears and hopes are only fancies' said a voice close to her, proceeding from a very shortsighted elderly man in spectacles who was sitting on a gnarled log. 'In running away you were acting on a conditioned reflex. It is quite

185

simple. Having lived among lions you have from your child-hood associated the sound of a roar with deadly danger. Hence your precipitate flight when that superstitious old jackass brayed at you. This remarkable discovery cost me twenty-five years of devoted research, during which I cut out the brains of innumerable dogs, and observed their spittle by making holes in their cheeks for them to salivate through instead of through their tongues. The whole scientific world is prostrate at my feet in admiration of this colossal achievement and gratitude for the light it has shed on the great problems of human conduct.'

'Why didnt you ask me?' said the black girl. 'I could have told you in twenty-five seconds without hurting those poor dogs.'

'Your ignorance and presumption are unspeakable' said the old myop. 'The fact was known of course to every child; but it had never been proved experimentally in the laboratory; and therefore it was not scientifically known at all. It reached me as an unskilled conjecture: I handed it on as science. Have you ever performed an experiment, may I ask?'

'Several' said the black girl. 'I will perform one now. Do you know what you are sitting on?'

'I am sitting on a log grey with age, and covered with an uncomfortable rugged bark' said the myop.

'You are mistaken' said the black girl. 'You are sitting on a sleeping crocodile.'

With a yell which Micah himself might have envied, the myop rose and fled frantically to a neighbouring tree, up which he climbed catlike with an agility which in so elderly a gentleman was quite superhuman.

'Come down' said the black girl. 'You ought to know that crocodiles are only to be found near rivers. I was only trying an experiment. Come down.'

'How am I to come down?' said the myop, trembling. 'I should break my neck.'

'How did you get up?' said the black girl.

'I dont know' he replied, almost in tears. 'It is enough to make a man believe in miracles. I couldnt have climbed this tree; and yet here I am and shall never be able to get down again.'

'A very interesting experiment, wasnt it?' said the black girl.

'A shamefully cruel one, you wicked girl' he moaned. 'Pray did it occur to you that you might have killed me? Do you suppose you can give a delicate physiological organism like mine a violent shock without the most serious and quite possibly fatal reactions on the heart? I shall never be able to sit on a log again as long as I live. I believe my pulse is quite abnormal, though I cannot count it; for if I let go of this branch I shall drop like a stone.'

'If you can cut half a dog's brain out without causing any reactions on its spittle you need not worry' she said calmly. 'I think African magic much more powerful than your divining by dogs. By saying one word to you I made you climb a tree like a cat. You confess it was a miracle.'

'I wish you would say another word and get me safely down again, confound you for a black witch' he grumbled.

'I will' said the black girl. 'There is a tree snake smelling at the back of your neck.'

The myop was on the ground in a jiffy. He landed finally on his back; but he scrambled to his feet at once and said 'You did not take me in: dont think it. I knew perfectly well you were inventing that snake to frighten me.'

'And yet you were as frightened as if it had been a real snake' said the black girl.

'I was not' said the myop indignantly. 'I was not frightened in the least.'

'You nipped down the tree as if you were' said the black girl.

'That is what is so interesting' said the myop, recovering his self-possession now that he felt safe. 'It was a conditioned reflex. I wonder could I make a dog climb a tree.'

'What for?' said the black girl.

'Why, to place this phenomenon on a scientific basis' said he.

'Nonsense!' said the black girl. 'A dog cant climb a tree.'

'Neither can I without the stimulus of an imaginary crocodile' said the professor. 'How am I to make a dog imagine a crocodile?'

'Introduce him to a few real ones to begin with' said the black girl.

'That would cost a good deal' said the myop, wrinkling his brows. 'Dogs are cheap if you buy them from professional dog-stealers, or lay in a stock when the dog tax becomes due; but crocodiles would run into a lot of money. I must think this out carefully.'

'Before you go' said the black girl 'tell me whether you believe in God.'

'God is an unnecessary and discarded hypothesis' said the myop. 'The universe is only a gigantic system of reflexes produced by shocks. If I give you a clip on the knee you will wag your ankle.'

'I will also give you a clip with my knobkerry; so dont do it' said the black girl.

'For scientific purposes it is necessary to inhibit such secondary and apparently irrelevant reflexes by tying the subject down' said the professor. 'Yet they also are quite relevant as examples of reflexes produced by association of ideas. I have spent twenty-five years studying their effects.'

'Effects on what?' said the black girl.

'On a dog's saliva' said the myop.

'Are you any the wiser?' she said.

'I am not interested in wisdom' he replied: 'in fact I do not know what it means and have no reason to believe that it exists. My business is to learn something that was not known before. I impart that knowledge to the world, and thereby add to the body of ascertained scientific truth.'

'How much better will the world be when it is all knowledge and no mercy?' said the black girl. 'Havent you brains enough to invent some decent way of finding out what you want to know?'

'Brains!' cried the myop, as if he could hardly believe his ears. 'You must be an extraordinarily ignorant young woman. Do you not know that men of science are all brains from head to foot?'

'Tell that to the crocodile' said the black girl.

By a well she meets also the kindly Jesus (called the conjurer) to whom she is attracted. She leaves him with reluctance when she finds that even he cannot give her satisfactory answers. But after further adventures with a caravan of white explorers, she comes upon Jesus once again. This time he is not alone.

She found a booth with many images of wood, plaster, or ivory set out for sale; and lying on the ground beside it was a big wooden cross on which the conjurer was lying with his ankles crossed and his arms stretched out. And the man who kept the booth was carving a statue of him in wood with great speed and skill. They were watched by a handsome Arab gentleman in a turban, with a scimitar in his sash, who was sitting on the coping of the well, and combing his beard.

'Why do you do this, my friend?' said the Arab gentleman. 'You know that it is a breach of the second commandment given by God to Moses. By rights I should smite you dead with my scimitar; but I have suffered and sinned all my life through an infirmity of spirit which renders me incapable of slaying any animal, even a man, in cold blood. Why do you do it?'

'What else can I do if I am not to starve?' said the conjurer. 'I am so utterly rejected of men that my only means of livelihood is to sit as a model to this compassionate artist who pays me sixpence an hour for stretching myself on this cross all day. He himself lives by selling images of me in this ridiculous position. People idolize me as the Dying Malefactor because they are interested in nothing but the police news. When he has laid in a sufficient stock of images, and I have saved a sufficient number of sixpences, I take a holiday and go about giving people good advice and telling them wholesome truths. If they would only listen to me they would be ever so much happier and better. But they refuse to believe me unless I do conjuring tricks for them; and when I do them they only throw me coppers and sometimes tickeys, and say what a wonderful man I am, and that there has been nobody like me ever on earth; but they go on being foolish and wicked and cruel all the same. It makes me feel that God has forsaken me sometimes.'

'What is a tickey?' said the Arab, rearranging his robe in more becoming folds.

'A threepenny bit' said the conjurer. 'It is coined because proud people are ashamed to be seen giving me coppers, and they think sixpence too much.'

'I should not like people to treat me like that' said the Arab. 'I also have a message to deliver. My people, if left to themselves, would fall down and worship all the images in that booth. If there were no images they would worship stones. My message is that there is no majesty and no might save in Allah the glorious, the great, the one and only. Of Him no mortal has ever dared to make an image: if anyone attempted such a crime I should forget that Allah is merciful, and overcome my infirmity to the extremity of slaying him with my own hand. But who could conceive the greatness of Allah in a bodily form? Not even an image of the finest horse could convey a notion of His beauty and greatness. Well, when I tell them this, they ask me, too, to do conjuring tricks; and when I tell them that I am a man like themselves and that not Allah Himself can violate His own laws – if one could conceive Him as doing anything unlawful – they go away and pretend that I am working miracles. But they believe; for if they doubt I have them slain by those who believe. That is what you should do, my friend.'

'But my message is that they should not kill one another' said the conjurer. 'One has to be consistent.'

'That is quite right as far as their private quarrels are concerned' said the Arab. 'But we must kill those who are unfit to live. We must weed the garden as well as water it.'

'Who is to be the judge of our fitness to live?' said the conjurer. 'The highest authorities, the imperial governors, and the high priests, find that I am unfit to live. Perhaps they are right.'

'Precisely the same conclusion was reached concerning myself' said the Arab. 'I had to run away and hide until I had convinced a sufficient number of athletic young men that their elders were mistaken about me: that, in fact, the boot was on the other leg. Then I returned with the athletic young men, and weeded the garden.'

'I admire your courage and practical sagacity' said the conjurer; 'but I am not built that way.'

'Do not admire such qualities' said the Arab. 'I am somewhat ashamed of them. Every desert chieftain displays them abundantly. It is on the superiority of my mind, which has made me the vehicle of divine inspiration, that I value myself. Have you ever written a book?'

'No' said the conjurer sadly: 'I wish I could; for then I could make money enough to come off this tiresome cross and send my message in print all over the world. But I am no author. I have composed a handy sort of short prayer with, I hope, all the essentials in it. But God inspires me to speak, not to write.'

'Writing is useful' said the Arab. 'I have been inspired to write many chapters of the word of Allah, praised be His name! But there are fellows in this world with whom Allah cannot be expected to trouble himself. His word means nothing to them; so when I have to deal with them I am no longer inspired, and have to rely on my own invention and my own wit. For them I write terrible stories of the Day of Judgment, and of the hell in which evildoers will suffer eternally. I contrast these horrors with enchanting pictures of the paradise maintained for those who do the will of Allah. Such a paradise as will tempt them, you understand: a paradise of gardens and perfumes and beautiful women.'

'And how do you know what is the will of Allah?' said the conjurer.

'As they are incapable of understanding it, my will must serve them for it instead' said the Arab. 'They can understand my will, which is indeed truly the will of Allah at second hand, a little soiled by my mortal passions and necessities, no doubt, but the best I can do for them. Without it I could not manage them at all. Without it they would desert me for the first chief who promised them a bigger earthly plunder. But what other chief can write a book and promise them an eternity of bliss after their death with all the authority of a mind which can surround its own inventions with the majesty of authentic inspiration?'

'You have every qualification for success' said the conjurer politely, and a little wistfully.

'I am the eagle and the serpent' said the Arab. 'Yet in my youth I was proud to be the servant of a widow and drive her camels. Now I am the humble servant of Allah and drive men for Him. For in no other do I recognize majesty and might; and with Him I take refuge from Satan and his brood.'

'What is all this majesty and might without a sense of beauty and the skill to embody it in images that time cannot change into corruption?' said the wood carver, who had been working and listening in silence. 'I have no use for your Allah, who forbids the making of images.'

'Know, dog of an unbeliever' said the Arab, 'that images have a power of making men fall down and worship them, even when they are images of beasts.'

'Or of the sons of carpenters' interjected the conjurer.

'When I drove the camels' continued the Arab, not quite catching the interruption 'I carried in my packs idols of men seated on thrones with the heads of hawks on their shoulders and scourges in their hands. The Christians who began by worshipping God in the form of a man, now worship him in the form of a lamb. This is the punishment decreed by Allah for the sin of presuming to imitate the work of His hands. But do not on that account dare to deny Allah His sense of beauty. Even your model here who is sharing your sin will remind you that the lilies of Allah are more lovely than the robes of Solomon in all his glory. Allah makes the skies His pictures and His children His statues, and does not withhold them from our earthy vision. He permits you to make lovely robes and saddles and trappings, and carpets to kneel on before Him, and windows like

flower beds of precious stones. Yet you will be meddling in
the work He reserves for Himself, and making idols. For
ever be such sin forbidden to my people!'

'Pooh!' said the sculptor 'your Allah is a bungler; and
he knows it. I have in my booth in a curtained-off corner
some Greek gods so beautiful that Allah himself may well
burst with envy when he compares them with his own
amateur attempts. I tell you Allah made this hand of mine
because his own hands are too clumsy, if indeed he have
any hands at all. The artist-god is himself an artist, never
satisfied with His work, always perfecting it to the limit of
His powers, always aware that though He must stop when
He reaches that limit, yet there is a further perfection without which the picture has no meaning. Your Allah can
make a woman. Can he make the Goddess of Love? No:
only an artist can do that. See!' he said, rising to go into his
booth. 'Can Allah make *her*?' And he brought from the
curtained corner a marble Venus and placed her on the
counter.

'Her limbs are cold' said the black girl, who had been
listening all this time unnoticed.

'Well said!' cried the Arab. 'A living failure is better
than a dead masterpiece; and Allah is justified against this
most presumptuous idolater, whom I must have slain with
a blow had you not slain him with a word.'

'I still live' said the artist, unabashed. 'That girl's limbs
will one day be colder than any marble. Cut my goddess in
two: she is still white marble to the core. Cut that girl in
two with your scimitar, and see what you will find there.'

'Your talk no longer interests me' said the Arab.
'Maiden: there is yet room in my house for another wife.
You are beautiful: your skin is like black satin: you are full
of life.'

'How many wives have you?' said the black girl.

'I have long since ceased to count them' replied the Arab; 'but there are enough to shew you that I am an experienced husband and know how to make women as happy as Allah permits.'

'I do not seek happiness: I seek God' said the black girl.

Weary of searching, she discovers at last the wise old gentleman (Voltaire) in his garden, and is joined (inevitably!) by the red-bearded Irishman.

Nothing particular happened after that until she came to a prim little villa with a very amateurish garden which was being cultivated by a wizened old gentleman whose eyes were so striking that his face seemed all eyes, his nose so remarkable that his face seemed all nose, and his mouth so expressive of a comically malicious relish that his face seemed all mouth until the black girl combined these three incompatibles by deciding that his face was all intelligence.

'Excuse me, baas' she said: 'may I speak to you?'

'What do you want?' said the old gentleman.

'I want to ask my way to God' she said; 'and as you have the most knowing face I have ever seen, I thought I would ask you.'

'Come in' said he. 'I have found, after a good deal of consideration, that the best place to seek God in is a garden. You can dig for Him here.'

'That is not my idea of seeking for God at all' said the black girl, disappointed. 'I will go on, thank you.'

'Has your own idea, as you call it, led you to Him yet?'

'No' said the black girl, stopping: 'I cannot say that it has. But I do not like your idea.'

'Many people who have found God have not liked Him and have spent the rest of their lives running away from him. Why do you suppose you would like him?'

'I don't know' said the black girl. 'But the missionary has a line of poetry that says that we needs must love the highest when we see it.'

'That poet was a fool' said the old gentleman. 'We hate it; we crucify it; we poison it with hemlock; we chain it to a stake and burn it alive. All my life I have striven in my little way to do God's work and teach His enemies to laugh at themselves; but if you told me God was coming down the road I should creep into the nearest mousehole and not dare to breathe until He had passed. For if He saw me or smelt me, might He not put His foot on me and squelch me, as I would squelch any venomous little thing that broke my commandments? These fellows who run after God crying "Oh that I knew where I might find Him," must have a tremendous opinion of themselves to think that they could stand before him. Has the missionary ever told you the story of Jupiter and Semele?'

'No' said the black girl. 'What is that story?'

'Jupiter is one of the names of God' said the old gentleman. 'You know that He has many names, dont you?'

'The last man I met called him Allah' she said.

'Just so' said the old gentleman. 'Well, Jupiter fell in love with Semele, and was considerate enough to appear and behave just like a man to her. But she thought herself good enough to be loved by a god in all the greatness of his godhood. So she insisted on his coming to her in the full panoply of his divinity.'

'What happened when he did?' asked the black girl.

'Just what she might have known would happen if she

had had any sense' said the old gentleman. 'She shrivelled up and cracked like a flea in the fire. So take care. Do not be a fool like Semele. God is at your elbow, and he has been there all the time; but in His divine mercy he has not revealed Himself to you lest too full a knowledge of Him should drive you mad. Make a little garden for yourself: dig and plant and weed and prune; and be content if he jogs your elbow when you are gardening unskilfully, and blesses you when you are gardening well.'

'And shall we never be able to bear His full presence?' said the black girl.

'I trust not' said the old philosopher. 'For we shall never be able to bear His full presence until we have fulfilled all His purposes and become gods ourselves. But as His purposes are infinite, and we are most briefly finite, we shall never, thank God, be able to catch up with His purposes. So much the better for us. If our work were done we should be of no further use: that would be the end of us; for He would hardly keep us alive for the pleasure of looking at us, ugly and ephemeral insects as we are. Therefore come in and help to cultivate this garden to His glory. The rest you had better leave to Him.'

So she laid down her knobkerry and went in and gardened with him. And from time to time other people came in and helped. At first this made the black girl jealous; but she hated feeling like that, and soon got used to their comings and goings.

One day she found a red haired Irishman labouring in the back garden where they grew the kitchen stuff.

'Who let you in here?' she said.

'Faith, I let meself in' said the Irishman. 'Why wouldnt I?'

'But the garden belongs to the old gentleman' said the black girl.

'I'm a Socialist' said the Irishman 'and dont admit that gardens belongs to annybody. That oul' fella is cracked and past his work and needs somewan to dig his podatoes for him. There's a lot been found out about podatoes since he learnt to dig them.'

'Then you did not come in to search for God?' said the black girl.

'Divvle a search' said the Irishman. 'Sure God can search for me if he wants me. My own belief is that he's not all that he sets up to be. He's not properly made and finished yet. There's somethin in us that's dhrivin at him, and somethin out of us that's dhrivin at him: that's certain; and the only other thing that's certain is that the somethin makes plenty of mistakes in thryin to get there. We'v got to find out its way for it as best we can, you and I; for there's a hell of a lot of other people thinkin of nothin but their own bellies.' And he spat on his hands and went on digging.

Both the black girl and the old gentleman thought the Irishman rather a coarse fellow (as indeed he was); but as he was useful and would not go away, they did their best to teach him nicer habits and refine his language. But nothing would ever persuade him that God was anything more solid and satisfactory than an eternal but as yet unfulfilled purpose, or that it could ever be fulfilled if the fulfilment were not made reasonably easy and hopeful by Socialism.

Still, when they had taught him manners and cleanliness they got used to him and even to his dreadful jokes. One day the old gentleman said to her 'It is not right that a fine young woman like you should not have a husband and children. I am much too old for you; so you had better marry that Irishman.'

As she had become very devoted to the old gentleman she was fearfully angry at first at his wanting her to marry anyone else, and even spent a whole night planning to drive the Irishman out of the place with her knobkerry. She could not bring herself to admit that the old gentleman had been born sixty years too early for her, and must in the course of nature die and leave her without a companion. But the old gentleman rubbed these flat facts into her so hard that at last she gave in; and the two went together into the kitchen garden and told the Irishman that she was going to marry him.

He snatched up his spade with a yell of dismay and made a dash for the garden gate. But the black girl had taken the precaution to lock it; and before he could climb it they overtook him and held him fast.

'Is it me marry a black heathen niggerwoman?' he cried piteously, forgetting all his lately acquired refinements of speech. 'Lemme go, will yous. I dont want to marry annywan.'

But the black girl held him in a grip of iron (softly padded, however); and the old gentleman pointed out to him that if he ran away he would only fall into the clutches of some strange woman who cared nothing about searching for God, and who would have a pale ashy skin instead of the shining black satin he was accustomed to. At last, after half an hour or so of argument and coaxing, and a glass of the old gentleman's best burgundy to encourage him, he said 'Well, I dont mind if I do.'

So they were married; and the black girl managed the Irishman and the children (who were charmingly coffee-coloured) very capably, and even came to be quite fond of them. Between them and the garden and mending her husband's clothes (which she could not persuade him to leave off wearing) she was kept so busy that her search for God was crowded out of her head most of the time; but there were moments, especially when she was drying her favourite piccaninny, who was very docile and quiet, after his bath, in which her mind went back to her search; only now she saw how funny it was that an unsettled girl should start off to pay God a visit, thinking herself the centre of the universe, and taught by the missionary to regard God as somebody who had nothing better to do than to watch everything she did and worry himself about her salvation. She even tickled the piccaninny and asked him 'Suppose I had found God at home what should I have done when he hinted that I was staying too long and that he had other things to attend to?' It was a question which the piccaninny was quite unable to answer: he only chuckled hysterically and tried to grab her wrists. It was only when the picca-ninnies grew up and became independent of her, and the Irishman had become an unconscious habit of hers, as if he were a part of herself, that they ceased to take her away from herself and she was left once more with the leisure and loneliness that threw her back on such questions. And by that time her strengthened mind had taken her far beyond the stage at which there is any fun in smashing idols with knobkerries.

[1932]

Letters to Dame Laurentia McLachlan

In April of 1924 Charlotte and Bernard Shaw first called on Dame Laurentia McLachlan at Stanbrook Abbey, near Worcester, the meeting having been prepared by their mutual friend, Sydney Cockerell. It began a quarter-century friendship, mostly carried on by correspondence, and often stormy. The most complete account is in the chapter called 'The Nun and the Dramatist' of the book, *In a Great Tradition*, which the Benedictines of Stanbrook issued after the Abbess's death (Harper's, 1956).

The Abbess, ten years Shaw's junior, knew little of Shaw's work before *Saint Joan*. But this she thought 'a wonderful play' though she took exception to some aspects of Joan's trial. Shaw found great delight in the fineness of her mind, and their extended arguments about Catholicism brought obvious enjoyment to them both. She was not prepared, however, for the 'blasphemy' of *The Adventures of the Black Girl*, and was sorrowfully shocked by Shaw's handling of the Christ figure and the use he made of the cross. She actually tried to persuade him to withdraw the book, and his refusal marked the beginning of a rift in their relations which lasted until 1934. Then Shaw misread an announcement of Dame Laurentia's fiftieth-year jubilee at Stanbrook as an announcement of her death, and wrote so movingly to her 'surviving' sisters that the 68-year-old Abbess, still vigorous, forgave the ageing playwright and resumed correspondence.

Or was the misreading deliberate? And did the sharp-eyed Abbess suspect as much? It is unlikely that we shall ever know. In any case here are two letters, one immediately before the rift, and one not long after the reconciliation, both adamant and full of guile in their effort to convert the devout nun to Shavianity.

The reference in the second letter is to *The Simpleton of the Unexpected Isles,* of which Shaw had sent her the proof sheets in January, 1935. The 'B.V.M.' is, of course, the Blessed Virgin Mary.

THE MALVERN HOTEL
GREAT MALVERN
July 24, 1933

Sister Laurentia,

You are the most unreasonable woman I ever knew. You want me to go out and collect 100,000 sold copies of *The Black Girl,* which have all been read and the mischief, if any, done; and then you want me to announce publicly that my idea of God Almighty is the antivegetarian deity who, after trying to exterminate the human race by drowning it, was coaxed out of finishing the job by a gorgeous smell of roast meat. Laurentia: has it never occurred to you that I might possibly have a more exalted notion of divinity, and that I dont as a matter of fact believe that Noah's deity ever existed or ever could exist? How could it possibly comfort you if I declared that I believed in him? It would simply horrify you. I know much better than you what you really believe. You think you believe the eighth chapter of Genesis; and I know you dont: if you did I would never speak to you again. You think you believe that Micah, when he wrote the eighth verse of his sixth chapter, was a liar and a blasphemer; but I know that you agree heartily with Micah, and that if you caught one of your nuns offering rams and calves and her first-born (if she had one) as a sacrifice to Jehovah you would have her out of the convent and into the nearest lunatic asylum before she could say Hail, Mary. You think you are a better Catholic than I; but my view of the Bible is the view of the Fathers of the Church; and yours is that of a Belfast Protestant to whom the Bible is a fetish and religion entirely irrational. You think you believe that God did not know what he was about when he made me and inspired me to write *The Black Girl*. For what happened was that when my wife was ill in Africa God came to me and said 'These women in Worcester plague me night and day with their prayers for you. What are you good for, anyhow?' So I said I could write a bit but was good for nothing else. God said then 'Take your pen and write what I shall put into your silly head.' When I had done so, I told you about it, thinking that you would be pleased, as it was the answer to your prayers. But you were not pleased at all, and peremptorily forbade me to publish it. So I went to God and said 'The Abbess is displeased.' And God said 'I am God; and I will not be trampled on by any Abbess that ever walked. Go and do as I have ordered you.' ... 'Well' I said 'I suppose I must publish the book if you are determined that I shall; but it will get me into trouble with the Abbess; for she is an obstinate unreasonable woman who will never let me take her out in my car; and there is no use your going to have a talk with her; for you might as well talk to the wall unless you let her have everything all her own way just as they taught it to her when she was a child.' So I leave you to settle it with God and his Son as best you can; but you must

203

go on praying for me, however surprising the result may be.

Your incorrigible

G. Bernard Shaw

UNION-CASTLE LINE

M.V. LLANGIBBY CASTLE

April 12, 1935

On the Equator. 82 in the shade. On the East coast of Africa. Cara Sorella Laurentia,

You are a puzzle to me with your unexpected rages. I ask myself, since I know that one becomes eminent in the Church through capacity for business more easily than by capacity for religion, 'Can Laurentia be a completely irreligious (or areligious) managing woman who becomes boss in a convent exactly as she would become boss in a castle or in a laundry?'

McLachlan? That suggests a clan of Covenanters to whom the worship of the B.V.M. is a damnable idolatry to be wiped out with claymore and faggot. Has Laurentia got that in her blood? If not, why in the name of all the saints does she fly out at me when I devoutly insist that the Godhead must contain the Mother as well as the Father?

Or is it merely personal? So many women hate their mothers (serve them right, mostly!) and see red when the cult of maternity arises.

You want me, as if it were a sort of penance, to say a lot of Hail Maries. But I am always saying Hail, Mary! on my travels. Of course I dont say it in that artificial form which means nothing. I say it in my own natural and sincere way when She turns up in the temples and tombs of Egypt and among the gods of Hindustan – Hallo, Mary! For you really cannot get away from Her. She has many names in the guide books, and many disguises. But She never takes me in. She favours Brother Bernardo with special revelations and smiles at his delighted 'Hallo, Mary!' When I write a play like *The Simpleton* and have to deal with divinity in it She jogs my elbow at the right moment and whispers 'Now Brother B. dont forget *me*.' And I dont.

But then you come along in a fury and cry 'How dare you? Cut all this stuff out, and say fifty Hail Maries.'

Which am I to obey? Our Lady of Stanbrook or Our Lady of Everywhere?

When you are old, as I am, these things will clear up and become real to you. I wonder whether, if Raphael had lived to be old like Michael Angelo, he would have given us something less absurd than the highly respectable Italian farmers' daughters he imposed so smugly on the world as visions of the B.V.M. Never have I stood before one of his Madonnas and exclaimed Hallo, Mary! Raphael made the adoration of the Mother impossible; but his view was so frankly and nicely human and fleshly and kindly that in the Dresden Madonna he produced for all time the ideal wet nurse, healthy, comely, and completely brainless.

On the other hand there is the giantess-goddess of Cimabue with her magnetic stare, a much deeper conception, but with just a little too much of the image and too little reality to be as approachable as the Egyptian goddesses of the great period.

In short, the Christian Maries are all failures. This suggests that the Jains were right in excluding God from their ritual as beyond human power to conceive or portray. At least that is their theory; but in practice they have in their shrines images of extraordinary beauty and purity of design who throw you into an ecstasy of prayer and a trance of peace when they look at you, as no Christian iconography can.

I said to the pundit who showed me round 'Those images are surely gods, are they not?' 'Not at all,' he said, 'they are statues of certain very wise men of the Jains.' This was obvious nonsense; so I pointed out that a man kneeling in the shrine (having first washed himself from head to foot) was clearly praying to a god. 'Pooh!' said the pundit with enormous contempt, 'he is only a heathen idolator.'

It is in these temples that you escape from the frightful parochiality of our little sects of Protestants and Catholics, and recognize the idea of God everywhere, and understand how the people who struggled hardest to establish the unity of God made the greatest number of fantastically different images of it, producing on us the effect of a crude polytheism.

Then comes the effort to humanize these images. The archaic Minerva becomes the very handsome and natural Venus of Milo. The Cimabue colossus becomes the wet nurse. Bellini's favourite model becomes as well known to us in her blue hood as any popular actress. Leonardo, Michael Angelo, Correggio (once, in the dome in Parma) lift these leading ladies, these stars of the studio, for a moment out of the hopelessly common; but on the whole, wisdom is with the Jains.

I have been getting into trouble by backing up a proposal to give Christ's Cathedral in Dublin to the Catholics, leaving St Patrick's to the Protestants. The two cathedrals are in a poor neighbourhood within a stone's throw of one another. St Patrick's was restored by Guinness the brewer, Christ's by Roe the distiller. The drunkenness of the poor Catholics paid`for both: why should they not have at least one?

But my own individual opinion is that cathedrals should be for all men, and not for this or that sect.

By this time we have passed the equator, and it is time for me to stop blaspheming.

Bless you, dear Laurentia.

G. Bernard Shaw

[1933–1935]

Preface to On the Rocks

As we have noted, Shaw was from youth fascinated by the story of Jesus's life and always frustrated when he thought in terms of dramatizing it. His blank-verse attempt at the age of twenty-two he abandoned before he reached the scene where Jesus was brought to Pilate. He could find no real drama in any of the passion plays – neither the one at Oberammergau nor the one written by John Masefield for performance in Canterbury Cathedral – *The Trial of Jesus*, 1925.

The following fragment which Shaw included in his Preface to *On the Rocks* in 1933 is not, it must be clearly understood, his notion of the Passion story. It is *what it would have been like* if Jesus had seen fit to defend himself – if he had been, in other words, a little more like Shaw himself.

Across the space of fifty-seven years there is little else that serves to connect Shaw's two attempts to put Jesus on the stage than his compulsion to cast himself in the rôle. One is forced to think of the conclusion of Colin Hurry's sonnet to Shaw:

> And yet, as if some memory compels
> Old thoughts from the subconscious undisguised
> The eyes betray the passion and the pain
> Of Jesus come again in cap and bells.

No man could expressly admit that his word would bring not peace but a sword without having satisfied himself that he was justified in doing so. He must have been told as frequently as I have been told that he was giving pain to many worthy people; and even with the fullest allowance for the strain of impishness with which the Life Force endows those of us who are destined by it to *épater le bourgeois*, he cannot have believed that the mere satisfaction of this Punchesque *Schadenfreude* could justify him in hurting anyone's feelings. What, then, would have been his defence if, at his trial, he had been his old self, defending himself as an accused man threatened with a horrible penalty, instead of a god going through an inevitable ordeal as a prelude to the establishment of his kingdom on earth?

A Modern Passion Play Impossible

The question is of such importance at the present crisis, when the kingdoms are breaking up, and upstart rulers are sowing their wild oats by such grotesque persecutions that Galileo's great successor Einstein is a plundered fugitive from officially threatened extermination, that I must endeavour to dramatize the trial of Jesus as it might have proceeded had it taken place before Peter uttered his momentous exclamation 'Thou art the Christ'. I have been asked repeatedly to dramatize the Gospel story, mostly by admirers of my dramatization of the trial of St Joan. But the trial of a dumb prisoner, at which the judge who puts the crucial question to him remains unanswered, cannot be dramatized unless the judge is to be the hero of the play. Now Pilate, though perhaps a trifle above the average of colonial governors, is not a heroic figure. Joan tackled her judges valiantly and wittily: her trial was a drama ready made, only needing to be brought within theatrical limits of time and space to be a thrilling play. But Jesus would not defend himself. It was not that he had not a word to say for himself, nor that he was denied the opportunity of saying it. He was not only allowed but challenged to defend himself. He was an experienced public speaker, able to hold multitudes with his oratory, happy and ready in debate and repartee, full of the illustrative hypothetical cases beloved of lawyers (called parables in the Gospels), and never at a loss when plied with questions. If ever there was a full dress debate for the forensic championship to be looked forward to with excited confidence by the disciples of the challenged expert it was this trial of Christ. Yet their champion put up no fight: he went like a lamb to the slaughter, dumb. Such a spectacle is disappointing on the stage, which is the one thing that a drama must not be; and when the disappointment is followed by scourging and crucifixion it is unbearable: not even the genius of our Poet Laureate, with all the magic of Canterbury Cathedral for scenery, can redeem it except for people who enjoy horror and catastrophe for their own sake and have no intellectual expectations to be disappointed.

Difference between Reader and Spectator

It may be asked why the incident of the trial and execution must fail on the stage, seeing that the gospel narrative is so pathetic, and so many of us have read it without disappointment. The answer is very simple: we have read it in childhood; and children go on from horror to horror breathlessly, knowing nothing of the constitutional questions at issue. Some of them remain in this condition of intellectual innocence to the end of their lives, whilst the cleverer ones seldom reconsider the impressions they have received as little children. Most Christians, I suspect, are afraid to think about it critically at all, having been taught to consider criticism blasphemous when applied to Bible stories. Besides, there are a thousand things that will pass in a well-told story that will not bear being brought to actuality on the stage. The evangelists can switch off our attention from Jesus to Peter hearing the cock crow (or the bugle blow) or to Pilate chaffering with the crowd about Barabbas; but on the stage the dumb figure cannot be got rid of: it is to him that we look for a speech that will take us up to heaven, and not to the weeping of Peter and the bawling of the mob, which become unbearable interruptions instead of skilful diversions.

For my part, when I read the story over again as an adult and as a professional critic to boot, I felt the disappointment so keenly that I have been ever since in the condition of the musician who, when he had gone to bed, heard somebody play an unresolved discord, and could not go to sleep until he had risen to play the resolution on his piano. What follows is my attempt to resolve Pilate's discord. I begin with the narrative of St John, the only one of the four which represents Jesus as saying anything more than any crazy person might in the same circumstances.

PILATE. Are you the king of the Jews?

JESUS. Do you really want to know? or have those people outside put it into your head to ask me?

PILATE. Am I a Jew, that I should trouble myself about you? Your own people and their priests have brought you to me for judgment. What have you done?

JESUS. My kingdom is not of this world: if it were, my followers would have fought the police and rescued me. But that sort of thing does not happen in my kingdom.

PILATE. Then you are a king?

JESUS. You say so. I came into this world and was born a common man for no other purpose than to reveal the truth.

And everyone capable of receiving the truth recognizes it in my voice.

PILATE. What is truth?

JESUS. You are the first person I have met intelligent enough to ask me that question.

PILATE. Come on! no flattery. I am a Roman, and no doubt seem exceptionally intelligent to a Jew. You Jews are always talking about truth and righteousness and justice: you feed on words when you are tired of making money, or too poor to have anything else to feed on. They want me to nail you up on a cross; but as I do not yet see what particular harm you have done I prefer to nail you down to an argument. Fine words butter no parsnips in Rome. You say your vocation is to reveal the truth. I take your word for it; but I ask you what is truth?

JESUS. It is that which a man must tell even if he be stoned or crucified for telling it. I am not offering you the truth at a price for my own profit: I am offering it freely to you for your salvation at the peril of my own life. Would I do that if I were not driven by God to do it against all the protests of my shrinking flesh?

PILATE. You Jews are a simple folk. You have found only one god. We Romans have found many; and one of them is a God of Lies. Even you Jews have to admit a Father of Lies whom you call the devil, deceiving yourselves with words as usual. But he is a very potent god, is he not? And as he delights not only in lies but in all other mischief such as stonings and crucifixions of innocent men, how am I to judge whether it is he who is driving you to sacrifice yourself for a lie, or Minerva driving you to be sacrificed for the truth? I ask you again, what is truth?

JESUS. It is what you know by your experience to be true or feel in your soul must be true.

PILATE. You mean that truth is a correspondence between

word and fact. It is true that I am sitting in this chair; but I am not the truth and the chair is not the truth: we are only the facts. My perception that I am sitting here may be only a dream; therefore my perception is not the truth.

JESUS. You say well. The truth is the truth and nothing else. That is your answer.

PILATE. Aye; but how far is it discoverable? We agree that it is true that I am sitting in this chair because our senses tell us so; and two men are not likely to be dreaming the same dream at the same moment. But when I rise from my chair this truth is no longer true. Truth is of the present, not of the future. Your hopes for the future are not the truth. Even in the present your opinions are not the truth. It is true that I sit in this chair. But is it true that it is better for your people that I should sit in this chair and impose on them the peace of Rome than that they should be left to slaughter oneanother in their own native savagery, as they are now clamouring to me to slaughter you?

JESUS. There is the peace of God that is beyond our understanding; and that peace shall prevail over the peace of Rome when God's hour strikes.

PILATE. Very pretty, my friend; but the hour of the gods is now and always; and all the world knows what the peace of your Jewish God means. Have I not read it in the campaigns of Joshua? We Romans have purchased the *pax Romana* with our blood; and we prefer it as a plain understandable thing which keeps men's knives off oneanother's throats to your peace which is beyond understanding because it slaughters man woman and child in the name of your God. But that is only our opinion. It is not yours. Therefore it is not necessarily the truth. I must act on it, because a governor must act on something: he cannot loaf round the roads and talk beautifully as you do. If you were a responsible governor instead of a poetic vagrant, you

213

would soon discover that my choice must lie, not between truth and falsehood, neither of which I can ever ascertain, but between reasonable and well informed opinion and sentimental and ill informed impulse.

JESUS. Nevertheless, opinion is a dead thing and impulse a live thing. You cannot impose on me with your reasonable and well informed opinion. If it is your will to crucify me, I can find you a dozen reasons for doing so; and your police can supply you with a hundred facts to support the reasons. If it is your will to spare me I can find you just as many reasons for that; and my disciples will supply you with more facts than you will have time or patience to listen to. That is why your lawyers can plead as well for one side as another, and can therefore plead without dishonour for the side that pays them, like the hackney charioteer who will drive you north as readily as south for the same fare.

PILATE. You are cleverer than I thought; and you are right. There is my will; and there is the will of Caesar to which my will must give way; and there is above Caesar the will of the gods. But these wills are in continual conflict with oneanother; therefore they are not truth; for truth is one, and cannot conflict with itself. There are conflicting opinions and conflicting wills; but there is no truth except the momentary truth that I am sitting in this chair. Yet you tell me that you are here to bear witness to the truth! You, a vagrant, a talker, who have never had to pass a sentence nor levy a tax nor issue an edict! What have you to say that I should not have the presumption scourged out of you by my executioners?

JESUS. Scourging is not a cure for presumption, nor is it justice, though you will perhaps call it so in your report to Caesar: it is cruelty; and that cruelty is wicked and horrible because it is the weapon with which the sons of Satan slay the sons of God is part of the eternal truth you seek.

PILATE. Leave out cruelty: all government is cruel; for nothing is so cruel as impunity. A salutary severity—

JESUS. Oh please! You must excuse me, noble Governor; but I am so made by God that official phrases make me violently sick. Salutary severity is ipecacuanha to me. I have spoken to you as one man to another, in living words. Do not be so ungrateful as to answer me in dead ones.

PILATE. In the mouth of a Roman words mean something: in the mouth of a Jew they are a cheap substitute for strong drink. If we allowed you you would fill the whole world with your scriptures and psalms and talmuds; and the history of mankind would become a tale of fine words and villainous deeds.

JESUS. Yet the word came first, before it was made flesh. The word was the beginning. The word was with God before he made us. Nay, the word was God.

PILATE. And what may all that mean, pray?

JESUS. The difference between man and Roman is but a word; but it makes all the difference. The difference between Roman and Jew is only a word.

PILATE. It is a fact.

JESUS. A fact that was first a thought; for a thought is the substance of a word. I am no mere chance pile of flesh and bone: if I were only that, I should fall into corruption and dust before your eyes. I am the embodiment of a thought of God: I am the Word made flesh: that is what holds me together standing before you in the image of God.

PILATE. That is well argued; but what is sauce for the goose is sauce for the gander; and it seems to me that if you are the Word made flesh so also am I.

JESUS. Have I not said so again and again? Have they not stoned me in the streets for saying it? Have I not sent my apostles to proclaim this great news to the Gentiles and to the very ends of the world? The Word is God. And God

is within you. It was when I said this that the Jews – my
own people – began picking up stones. But why should you,
the Gentile, reproach me for it?

PILATE. I have not reproached you for it. I pointed it out
to you.

JESUS. Forgive me. I am so accustomed to be contradicted—

PILATE. Just so. There are many sorts of words; and they
are all made flesh sooner or later. Go among my soldiers
and you will hear many filthy words and witness many
cruel and hateful deeds that began as thoughts. I do not
allow those words to be spoken in my presence. I punish
those deeds as crimes. Your truth, as you call it, can be
nothing but the thoughts for which you have found words
which will take effect in deeds if I set you loose to scatter
your words broadcast among the people. Your own people
who bring you to me tell me that your thoughts are abomin-
able and your words blasphemous. How am I to refute
them? How am I to distinguish between the blasphemies of
my soldiers reported to me by my centurions and your
blasphemies reported to me by your High Priest?

JESUS. Woe betide you and the world if you do not distinguish!

PILATE. So you think. I am not frightened. Why do you
think so?

JESUS. I do not think: I know. I have it from God.

PILATE. I have the same sort of knowledge from several
gods.

JESUS. In so far as you know the truth you have it from
my God, who is your heavenly father and mine. He has
many names and his nature is manifold. Call him what you
will: he is still Our Father. Does a father tell his children
lies?

PILATE. Yes: many lies. You have an earthly father and

an earthly mother. Did they tell you what you are preaching?

JESUS. Alas! no.

PILATE. Then you are defying your father and mother. You are defying your Church. You are breaking your God's commandments, and claiming a right to do so. You are pleading for the poor, and declaring that it is easier for a camel to pass through the eye of a needle than for a rich man to enter your God's paradise. Yet you have feasted at the tables of the rich, and encouraged harlots to spend on perfume for your feet money that might have been given to the poor, thereby so disgusting your treasurer that he has betrayed you to the High Priest for a handful of silver. Well, feast as much as you please: I do not blame you for refusing to play the fakir and make yourself a walking exhibition of silly austerities; but I must draw the line at your making a riot in the temple and throwing the gold of the moneychangers to be scrambled for by your partisans. I have a law to administer. The law forbids obscenity, sedition, and blasphemy. You are accused of sedition and blasphemy. You do not deny them: you only talk about the truth, which turns out to be nothing but what you like to believe. Your blasphemy is nothing to me: the whole Jewish religion is blasphemy from beginning to end from my Roman point of view; but it means a great deal to the High Priest; and I cannot keep order in Jewry except by dealing with Jewish fools according to Jewish folly. But sedition concerns me and my office very closely; and when you undertook to supersede the Roman Empire by a kingdom in which you and not Caesar are to occupy the throne, you were guilty of the uttermost sedition. I am loth to have you crucified; for though you are only a Jew, and a half baked young one at that, yet I perceive that you are in your Jewish way a man of quality; and it makes me uneasy to throw a

man of quality to the mob, even if his quality be only a
Jewish quality. For I am a patrician and therefore myself a
man of quality; and hawks should not pick out hawks' eyes.
I am actually condescending to parley with you at this
length in the merciful hope of finding an excuse for tolerating your blasphemy and sedition. In defence you offer me
nothing but an empty phrase about the truth. I am sincere
in wishing to spare you; for if I do not release you I shall
have to release that blackguard Barabbas, who has gone
further than you and killed somebody, whereas I understand that you have only raised a Jew from the dead. So for
the last time set your wits to work, and find me a sound
reason for letting a seditious blasphemer go free.

JESUS. I do not ask you to set me free; nor would I accept
my life at the price of Barabbas's death even if I believed
that you could countermand the ordeal to which I am predestined. Yet for the satisfaction of your longing for the
truth I will tell you that the answer to your demand is your
own argument that neither you nor the prisoner whom you
judge can prove that he is in the right; therefore you must
not judge me lest you be yourself judged. Without sedition
and blasphemy the world would stand still and the Kingdom of God never be a stage nearer. The Roman Empire
began with a wolf suckling two human infants. If these
infants had not been wiser than their fostermother your
empire would be a pack of wolves. It is by children who are
wiser than their fathers, subjects who are wiser than their
emperors, beggars and vagrants who are wiser than their
priests, that men rise from being beasts of prey to believing
in me and being saved.

PILATE. What do you mean by believing in you?

JESUS. Seeing the world as I do. What else could it mean?

PILATE. And you are the Christ, the Messiah, eh?

JESUS. Were I Satan, my argument would still hold.

PILATE. And I am to spare and encourage every heretic, every rebel, every lawbreaker, every rapscallion lest he should turn out to be wiser than all the generations who made the Roman law and built up the Roman Empire on it?

JESUS. By their fruits ye shall know them. Beware how you kill a thought that is new to you. For that thought may be the foundation of the kingdom of God on earth.

PILATE. It may also be the ruin of all kingdoms, all laws, and all human society. It may be the thought of the beast of prey striving to return.

JESUS. The beast of prey is not striving to return: the kingdom of God is striving to come. The empire that looks back in terror shall give way to the kingdom that looks forward with hope. Terror drives men mad: hope and faith give them divine wisdom. The men whom you fill with fear will stick at no evil and perish in their sin: the men whom I fill with faith shall inherit the earth. I say to you Cast out fear. Speak no more vain things to me about the greatness of Rome. The greatness of Rome, as you call it, is nothing but fear: fear of the past and fear of the future, fear of the poor, fear of the rich, fear of the High Priests, fear of the Jews and Greeks who are learned, fear of the Gauls and Goths and Huns who are barbarians, fear of the Carthage you destroyed to save you from your fear of it and now fear worse than ever, fear of imperial Caesar, the idol you have yourself created, and fear of me, the penniless vagrant, buffeted and mocked, fear of everything except the rule of God: faith in nothing but blood and iron and gold. You, standing for Rome, are the universal coward: I, standing for the kingdom of God, have braved everything, lost everything, and won an eternal crown.

PILATE. You have won a crown of thorns; and you shall wear it on the cross. You are a more dangerous fellow than

219

I thought. For your blasphemy against the god of the high priests I care nothing: you may trample their religion into hell for all I care; but you have blasphemed against Caesar and against the Empire; and you mean it, and have the power to turn men's hearts against it as you have half turned mine. Therefore I must make an end of you whilst there is still some law left in the world.

JESUS. Law is blind without counsel. The counsel men agree with is vain: it is only the echo of their own voices. A million echoes will not help you to rule righteously. But he who does not fear you and shews you the other side is a pearl of the greatest price. Slay me and you go blind to your damnation. The greatest of God's names is Counsellor; and when your Empire is dust and your name a byword among the nations the temples of the living God shall still ring with his praise as Wonderful! Counsellor! the Everlasting Father, the Prince of Peace.

[1933]

'In Good King Charles's Golden Days'

After Shaw had been involved in the defence of some conscientious objectors in World War I, he became quite interested in the Quakers, as was evident in his essay *On Ritual, Religion, and the Intolerableness of Tolerance*, and frequently described himself as a kind of Quaker. He did not, however, attend Friends' Meetings, and Friends themselves have never come forward to claim him. Part of his enthusiasm for the Society emanated from his admiration of its founder, George Fox, whose *Journal* he must have read. He had considered writing a play about Fox, but seems to have abandoned the idea when he gave his attention to another mystic, Joan of Arc.

Finally, in his eighties, he included Fox in the seventeenth-century conversation piece, *'In Good King Charles's Golden Days'*, along with some other contemporary favourites: the painter, Godfrey Kneller, Newton, Charles II and his mistresses. Most of this 'true history that never happened' is a series of improbable intrusions on the privacy of Isaac Newton. Charles, George Fox, Nell Gwynn, Barbara Villiers, have already assaulted Newton's housekeeper, Mrs Basham, when a near-by church bell sounds. . . .

He is interrupted by the clangour of a church bell, which has a terrible effect on him.

FOX [*in a thundering voice, forgetting all about the duchess*] Ha! I am called: I must go.

He makes for the door but is stopped by Charles, who, releasing Nell, shuts it quickly and posts himself with his back to it.

CHARLES. Stop. You are going to brawl in church. You will be thrown into prison; and I shall not be able to save you.

FOX. The bell, the bell. It strikes upon my life. I am called. Earthly kings cannot stay me. Let me pass.

CHARLES. Stand back, Mr Fox. My person is sacred.

NEWTON. What is the matter?

CHARLES. The church bell: it drives him mad. Someone send and stop it.

The bell stops.

FOX. God has stopped it. [*He falls on his knees and collapses, shivering like a man recovering from a fit.*]

Charles and Newton help him to his feet and lead him back to his chair.

FOX [*to Charles*] Another stroke, and I should not have answered for your life.

BARBARA. You must control yourself, preacher. In any decent English village you would be put in the stocks to teach you good manners.

FOX. Woman: I have been put in the stocks; and I shall be put there again. But I will continue to testify against the steeple house and the brazen clangour of its belfries.

MRS BASHAM. Now Mr Fox. You must not say such things here.

FOX. I tell you that from the moment you allow this man-made monster called a Church to enter your mind your inner light is like an extinguished candle; and your soul is plunged in darkness and damned. There is no atheist like the Church atheist. I have converted many a poor atheist who would have been burnt or hanged if God had not sent him into my hands; but I have never converted a churchman: his answer to everything is not his God, but the Church, the Church, the Church. They burn each other, these churchmen: they persecute: they do wickednesses of which no friend of God would be capable.

MRS BASHAM. The Popish Church, not the Protestant one, Mr Fox.

FOX. All, all, all of them. They are all snares of the devil. They stand between Man and his Maker, and take on themselves divine powers when they lack divine attributes. Am I to hold my peace in the face of this iniquity? When the bell rings to announce some pitiful rascal twaddling in his pulpit, or some fellow in a cassock pretending to bind and loose, I hear an Almighty Voice call 'George Fox, George Fox: rise up: testify: unmask these impostors: drag them down from their pulpits and their altars; and let it be known that what the world needs to bring it back to God is not Churchmen but Friends, Friends of God, Friends of man, friendliness and sincerity everywhere, superstition and pulpit play-acting nowhere.'

CHARLES. Pastor: it is not given to every man as it has been to you to make a religion for himself. A readymade Church is an indispensable convenience for most of us. The inner light must express itself in music, in noble architecture, in eloquence: in a word, in beauty, before it can pass into the minds of common men. I grant you the clergy are mostly dull dogs; but with a little disguise and ritual they will pass as holy men with the ignorant. And there are great mysteries that must be symbolized, because though we feel them we do not know them, Mr Newton having not yet discovered their nature, in spite of all his mathematics. And this reminds me that we are making a most unwarrantable intrusion on our host's valuable time. Mr Newton: on my honour I had no part in bringing upon you this invasion of womanhood. I hasten to take them away, and will wait upon you at some happier moment. Come, ladies: we must leave Mr Newton to his mathematics. [*He is about to go to the door. Barbara rises to accompany him.*]

NEWTON [*stopping him*] I must correct that misunderstanding, sir. I would not have you believe that I could be so inhospitable as to drive away my guests merely to indulge in the trifling pursuit of mathematical calculation, which leads finally nowhere. But I have more serious business in hand this morning. I am engaged in a study of the prophecies in the book of Daniel. [*He indicates the Bible.*] It may prove of the greatest importance to the world. I beg you to allow me to proceed with it in the necessary solitude. The ladies have not wasted my time: I have to thank her Grace of Cleveland for some lights on the Book of Revelation suggested to me by her proceedings. But solitude – solitude absolutely free from the pleasant disturbance of ladies' society – is now necessary to me; and I must beg you to withdraw.

They are interrupted by the entrance of yet another of Charles's ladies, Louise de Keroualle, who wishes to consult Newton as an 'alchemist'.

FOX. Would you endanger your souls by dabbling in magic? The scripture says 'Thou shalt not suffer a witch to live.' Do you think that God is fonder of sorcerers and wizards than of witches? If you count the wrath of God as nothing, and are above the law by your rank, are you not ashamed to believe such old wives' tales as the changing of lead into gold by the philosopher's stone?

NEWTON. Pastor Fox: I thank you for your wellmeant warning. Now let me warn you. The man who begins by doubting the possibility of the philosopher's stone soon finds himself beginning to doubt the immortality of the soul. He ends by doubting the existence of the soul. There is no witchcraft about these things. I am as certain of them as I am of the fact that the world was created four thousand and four years before the birth of our Lord.

FOX. And what warrant have you for that? The Holy Bible says nothing of your four thousand and four. It tells us that the world was created 'in the beginning': a mighty word. 'In the beginning'! Think of it if you have any imagination. And because some fool in a steeplehouse, dressed up like a stage player in robes and mitre, dares to measure the days of the Almighty by his kitchen clock, you take his word before the word of God! Shame on you, Isaac Newton, for making an idol of an archbishop! There is no credulity like the credulity of philosophers.

NEWTON. But the archbishop has counted the years! My own chronology of the world has been founded on his calculation. Do you mean to tell me that all the labour I have bestowed on that book has been wasted?

FOX. Sinfully wasted.

NEWTON. George Fox: you are an infidel. Leave my house.

FOX [rising] Your philosophy has led you to the conclusion that George Fox is an infidel. So much the worse for your philosophy! The Lord does not love men that count numbers. Read second Samuel, chapter twentyfour: the book is before you. Good morning; and God bless you and enlighten you. [He turns to go.]

CHARLES. Stay, Pastor. [*He makes Fox sit down again and goes to Newton, laying a hand on his shoulder.*] Mr Newton: the word infidel is not one to be used hastily between us three. Old Tom Hobbes, my tutor, who was to me what Aristotle was to Alexander the Great, was called an infidel. You yourself, in spite of your interest in the book of Daniel, have been suspected of doubting whether the apple falls from the tree by the act of God or by a purely physical attraction. Even I, the head of the Church, the Defender of the Faith, stand between the Whigs who suspect me of being a Papist and the Tories who suspect me of being an atheist. Now the one thing that is true of all three of us is that if the common people knew our real minds they would hang us and bury us in unconsecrated ground. We must stand together, gentlemen. What does it matter to us whether the world is four thousand years old, or, as I should guess, ten thousand?

NEWTON. The world ten thousand years old! Sir: you are mad.

NELL [*shocked*] Rowley darling: you mustnt say such things.

BARBARA. What business is it of yours, pray? He has always defied God and betrayed women. He does not know the meaning of the word religion. He laughed at it in France. He hated it in Scotland. In England he believes nothing. He loves nothing. He fears nothing except having to go on his travels again, as he calls it. What are ten thousand years to him, or ten million?

FOX. Are ten million years beyond the competence of Almighty God? They are but a moment in His eyes. Four thousand years seem an eternity to a mayfly, or a mouse, or a mitred fool called an archbishop. Are we mayflies? Are we mice? Are we archbishops?

MRS BASHAM. Mr Fox: I have listened to too much

226

blasphemy this morning. But to call an archbishop a mitred fool and compare him to a mouse is beyond endurance. I cannot believe that God will ever pardon you for that. Have you no fear of hell?

FOX. How shall I root out the sin of idolatry from this land? Worship your God, woman, not a dressed-up priest.

MRS BASHAM. The archbishop is not a graven image. And when he is officiating he is not in the likeness of anything in the heavens above or on the earth beneath. I am afraid you do not know your catechism, Mr Fox.

CHARLES [*laughing*] Excellent, Mrs Basham. Pastor: she has gravelled you with the second commandment. And she has put us to shame for quarrelling over a matter of which we know nothing. By the way, where were we when we began to quarrel? I have clean forgotten.

[1939]

Preface to Farfetched Fables

As I have now entered my 93rd year, my fans must not expect from me more than a few crumbs dropped from the literary loaves I distributed in my prime, plus a few speculations as to what may happen in the next million light years that are troubling me in the queer second wind that follows second childhood.

*   *   *

All I can plead is that as events as they actually occur mean no more than a passing crowd to a policeman on point duty, they must be arranged in some comprehensible order as stories. Without this there can be no history, no morality, no social conscience. Thus the historian, the story teller, the playwright and his actors, the poet, the mathematician, and the philosopher, are functionaries without whom civilization would not be possible. I conclude that I was born a story teller because one was needed. I am therefore not a disease but a social necessity.

Providence, which I call The Life Force, when not defeated by the imperfection of its mortal instruments, always takes care that the necessary functionaries are born specialized for their job. When no specialization beyond that of common mental ability is needed, millions of 'hands' (correctly so called industrially) are born. But as they are helpless without skilled craftsmen and mechanics, without directors and deciders, without legislators and thinkers, these also are provided in the required numbers. Chaucer and Shakespear, Dante and Michael Angelo, Goethe and Ibsen, Newton and Einstein, Adam Smith and Karl Marx arrive only once at intervals of hundreds of years, whilst carpenters and tailors, stockbrokers and parsons, industrialists and traders are all forthcoming in thousands as fast as they are needed.

I present myself therefore as an instrument of the Life Force, writing by what is called inspiration; but as the Life Force proceeds experimentally by Trial-and-Error, and never achieves a 100 per cent success, I may be one of its complete failures, and certainly fall very short not only of perfection but of the Force's former highest achievements. For instance I am much less mentally gifted than, say, Leibniz, and can only have been needed because, as he was so gifted as to be unintelligible to the mob, it remained for some simpler soul like myself to translate his nomads and his universal substance, as he called the Life Force, into fables which, however farfetched, can at least interest, amuse, and perhaps enlighten those capable of such entertainment, but baffled by Leibniz's algebraic symbols and his philosophic jargon.

Here I must warn you that you can make no greater mistake in your social thinking than to assume, as too many do, that persons with the rarest mental gifts or specific talents are in any other respect superior beings. The Life Force, when it gives some needed extraordinary quality to some individual, does not bother about his or her morals. It may even, when some feat is required which a human being can perform only after drinking a pint of brandy, make him a dipsomaniac, like Edmund Kean, Robson, and

Dickens on his last American tour. Or, needing a woman capable of bearing first rate children, it may endow her with enchanting sexual attraction yet leave her destitute of the qualities that make married life with her bearable. Apparently its aim is always the attainment of power over circumstances and matter through science, and is to this extent benevolent; but outside this bias it is quite unscrupulous, and lets its agents be equally so. Geniuses are often spendthrifts, drunkards, libertines, liars, dishonest in money matters, backsliders of all sorts, whilst many simple credulous souls are models of integrity and piety, high in the calendar of saints.

* * *

As it is, Christianity has split into sects, persuasions, and Nonconformities in all directions. The Statesman's Year-Book has given up trying to list them. They range from Pillars of Fire, Jehovah's Witnesses, Plymouth Brothers, and Glasites, to Presbyterians, Methodists, Congregationalists, Baptists, Friends (Quakers), and Unitarians. Within the Established Church itself there are Ritualists, Anglo-Catholics who call their services Masses and never mention the Reformation, Laodicean Broad Churchmen, and Low Church Protestants. The Friends abhor ritual and dictated prayers, and repudiate cathedral services and Masses as playacting, whilst the Anglo-Catholics cannot think religiously without them. Presbyterians and Congregationalists differ from the clergy of the Established Church on the political issue of episcopal or lay Church government. The Unitarians reject the Trinity and deny deity to Jesus. Calvinists deny universal atonement, preached by our missionaries, who are practically all Independents.

Common to these irreconcilable faiths is the pretension that each is the true Catholic Church, and should hand over all whom it cannot convert to the State (the Secular Arm) to be exterminated for the crime of heresy by the cruellest possible methods, even to burning alive. This does not mean that all rulers who order such extermination are horribly cruel. 'Bloody Mary' believed that heretics must be liquidated; but she was not responsible for the political circumstance that the secular criminal law was atrociously cruel, and that no other agency could effect the liquidation. Calvin agreed that Servetus must be killed; but he objected humanely to his being burned. Charles II, humane (indeed, as some think, too humane in his kindness to his dozen dogs and half-dozen mistresses), could not question the necessity for punishing the Regicides with death; but he loathed the butchering of them in the hideous manner ordained centuries earlier for the punishment of William Wallace, and stopped it as soon as he dared. It was still unrepealed during my own lifetime; and has only just (1948) been repealed in Scotland.

So far I have not been imprisoned, as poorer men have been in my time, for blasphemy or apostasy. I am not technically an apostate, as I have never been confirmed; and my godparents are dead. But having torn some of the Thirtynine Articles to rags, I should have been pilloried and had my ears cropped had I lived in the days of the British Inquisition called the Star Chamber. Nowadays Nonconformity and Agnosticism are far too powerful electorally for such persecution. But the Blasphemy Laws are still available and in use against obscure sceptics, whilst I suffer nothing worse than incessant attempts to convert me. All the religions and their sects, Christian or Moslem, Buddhist or Shinto, Jain or Jew, call me to repentance, and ask me for subscriptions. I am not so bigoted as to dismiss their experiences as the inventions of liars and the fancies of noodles. They are evidence like any other human evidence;

231

and they force me to the conclusion that every grade of human intelligence can be civilized by providing it with a frame of reference peculiar to its mental capacity, and called a religion.

*   *   *

It may seem that between a Roman Catholic who believes devoutly in Confession and a modern freethinking scientist there can be neither sympathy nor co-operation. Yet there is no essential difference between Confession and modern Psychotherapy. The post-Freudian psychoanalyst relieves his patient of the torments of guilt and shame by extracting a confession of their hidden cause. What else does the priest do in the confessional, though the result is called cure by one and absolution by the other? What I, a Freethinker, call the Life Force, my pious neighbours call Divine Providence: in some respects a better name for it. Bread and wine are changed into living tissue by swallowing and digestion. If this is not transubstantiation what *is* transubstantiation? I have described the surprise of a Fabian lecturer on being asked to open a political meeting with prayer. When I was invited to address the most important Secular Society in England I found that I had to supply the sermon in a ritual of hymns and lessons in all respects like a religious Sunday service except that the lessons were from Browning and the hymns were aspirations to 'join the choir invisible'. Later on, when I attended a church service in memory of my wife's sister, and was disposed to be moved by it, the lesson was the chapter from the Bible which describes how the Israelites in captivity were instructed by a deified Jonathan Wild to steal the jewelry of the Egyptians before their flight into the desert. The Leicester Atheists were in fact more pious than the Shropshire Anglicans.

[1948–1949]

Sixteen Self Sketches

At ninety-three there is nothing left to say that has not
been said before, but in the little volume of *Sixteen Self
Sketches* in 1949 he reviews 'What Is My Religious
Faith?'

What then am I, an artist-biologist, to call myself when
asked to define my religion? I am a Catholic because I am
a Communist (the two words mean the same) intelligent
enough to perceive that our civilization, such as it is, could
not exist for a week without its vast Communist basis of
policed roads and bridges, water supplies and street lamps,
courts of justice, schools, churches, legislatures, administra-
tions, common and statutory law, armies, navies, air forces,
etc., all staring in the faces of the ignorant majority of
people to whom Communist is only a term of vulgar abuse,
and Communism an epitome of everything evil and in
famous. But if I call myself a Catholic I am taken to be a
member of one or other of the established Christian
Churches, all self-styled Catholic, whether Roman, Anglican, Greek, or what not, and all saturated with opiate fancies
such as the Atonement, dear to the dishonest who, dreading
the bugbear of a brimstone hell, dare not sin for six days
without being washed clean in the blood of the Lamb on
the seventh, and all clinging to a fiction of personal immor-

tality, which anæsthetizes the fear of death for the average man. 'The average man is a coward' said Mark Twain.

As to the cardinal Christian precept 'Love one another' I, contemplating humanity in the persons of a few rich ladies and gentlemen confronted by a multitude of poor working folk, glorying in warfare, and wallowing in superstition, not only do not love them but dislike them so much that they must be replaced by more sensible animals if civilization is to be saved. I really cannot love Hitlers and Pavlovs and their idolaters any more than I could have loved the saintly Torquemada or the æsthetic Nero.

If I call myself a Vitalist I shall be classed as a Materialist by the scientists who admit the existence of a life force but conceive it as purely mechanical like steam or electricity.

If I call myself simply an Evolutionist I shall be listed as a Darwinian. Yet if I repudiate Darwin it will be assumed that I attach no importance to the part played in human destiny by Natural Selection and by Reason; for the popular imagination works only in extremes: soot or whitewash, Right or Left, white or black. I am neither white nor black, but a classical grey, being very ignorant. All cats are grey in the dark.

I do not accept even the almost unquestioned sequence of Cause and Effect. It is the other way about with me. Bar pure accident, it is the aim, the purpose, the intended effect, that produces its so-called cause. If I shoot my neighbour it is not the fault of my gun and its trigger, nor is the rope the cause of my execution. Both are the effects of my intention to murder and the jury's sense of justice.

And so, as Bergson is the established philosopher of my sect, I set myself down as a Creative Evolutionist. And at that I should leave it, being too old a dog to pick up new tricks, were it not that I am still asked where God comes into my religion. When I parry such questions by 'Where

234

does He come into yours?' the two replies come to the same. The Churches have to postulate a God Almighty who, obviously, is either not almighty or not benevolent; for the world is crowded with evil as much as with good to such an extent that many of its ablest thinkers, from Ecclesiastes to Shakespear, have been pessimists; and the optimists have had to postulate a devil as well as a god. Both have had to reckon with the operation of a natural agency which the Churches call Providence and the scientists Phlogiston, Functional Adaptation, Natural Selection, Vis Naturae Medicatrix, the Necessary Myth, and Design in the Universe. I have called it the Life Force and the Evolutionary Appetite. Bergson called it the *Élan Vitale*, Kant the Categorical Imperative, Shakespear the 'divinity that shapes our ends, rough-hew them how we will'. They all come to the same thing: a mysterious drive towards greater power over our circumstances and deeper understanding of Nature, in pursuit of which men and women will risk death as explorers or martyrs, and sacrifice their personal comfort and safety against all prudence, all probability, all common sense.

As this unaccountable agency confronts every religion alike as a hard fact in spite of its many different names, it might as well be called Providence, which is the most expressive vernacular word for it. Thus much of the difference between the crudest Evangelism and Creative Evolution is found in administrative practice to be imaginary. Certainly the Bible Gods, of whom there are at least five, are all held on paper to be almighty, infallible, omnipotent and omniscient, whereas the Life Force, however benevolent, proceeds by trial and error and creates the problem of evil by its unsuccessful experiments and its mistakes. No practical administrative authority has ever been able to function on the assumption that almighty power, infallibility, and

235

omniscience exist, or have ever existed or will exist in the world. When an atheist becomes a Plymouth Brother, or vice versa, the final comment is *plus ça change, plus c'est la même chose*. The infallibility of God is a fiction that may be as necessary politically as the infallibility of the Pope or of the Judicial Committee of the House of Lords; but it is a fiction all the same.

It matters hardly at all what our denominations are; and I must disclaim any design to impose my denomination on others. I do not forget the warning of Jesus that if we try to clear established religions of their weeds we may pull up the wheat as well and leave the husbandmen without any religion. I detest the doctrine of the Atonement, holding that ladies and gentlemen cannot as such possibly allow anyone else to expiate their sins by suffering a cruel death. But I know as a hard fact that Methodism, which is saturated with this abhorrent superstition, changed our colliers and their wives and mothers from savages into comparatively civilized beings; and that any attempt to convert them to Creative Evolution would have made them more dangerous savages than ever, with no scruples, no personal god (the only sort of God they could believe in), and no fear of hell to restrain them. To change a credulous peasantry to a sceptical one by inculcating a negative atheism plus a science beyond the reaches of their brains may make an end of civilization, not for the first time. It may even make an end of mankind, as it has already made an end of diplodoccus and dinosaur, mammoth and mastodon. Creative Evolution can replace us; but meanwhile we must work for our survival and development as if we were Creation's last word. Defeatism is the wretchedest of policies.

[1949]

236

Notes on the Sources of the Selections

Where possible the editor has used the text of the *Standard Edition* of the Collected Works published by Constable and Co., Ltd. Items marked with an asterisk (*) were included in the folder labelled 'Religion and Religions', British Museum 50663.

On Going to Church appeared in the first issue of *The Savoy*, January, 1896. Only the latter part of the essay is used here. It may be found complete in *The Savoy, Nineties Experiment*, edited by Stanley Weintraub (Pennsylvania State University Press, University Park, 1965), p. 3. The Shaw Society (45 Steeplestone Close, London, N.18) has also reissued this essay as Shavian Tract No. 5, December, 1957.

Man and Superman, including the Preface, was first printed in 1903. The quotations are from the Standard Edition (1931) pp. xx–xxv, and xxxi–xxxiii. The passage from the play is on pp. 126–9.

John Bull's Other Island was first printed in 1907 with *How He Lied to Her Husband* and *Major Barbara*. The selections are from the Standard Edition (1931) pp. 149–52 and 175–8.

Major Barbara was part of the above publication. The passage quoted is on pp. 338–40.

On Miracles: A Retort – originally *A Retort on Mr Chesterton* – appeared in *The New Age*, 10 December 1908, pp. 129–30.

The Shewing-Up of Blanco Posnet was first printed in 1911. In the Standard Edition (combined with *The Doctor's Dilemma*

237

and *Getting Married,* 1932) Blanco's sermon is on pp. 454–457.

**God Must Be Non-Sectarian and International* appeared as a letter to *The Christian Commonwealth* of 17 July 1912, p. 683. It was headed, 'The Idea of God./Mr G. Bernard Shaw's Surrejoinder to Mr Campbell.'

Common Sense About the War appeared in *The New Statesman* for 14 November 1914. With the other war-time essays and letters-to-the-editor it was reprinted in *What I Really Wrote About the War* (New York, 1932) in which the section quoted appears on pp. 83–5.

On the Prospects of Christianity, as the Preface to *Androcles and the Lion,* was first published in 1916 with *Overruled* and *Pygmalion.* They are similarly grouped in the Standard Edition (1931), from which the passages quoted were excerpted: pp. 3–6; 33–7; and 44–51.

**Quot Homines, Tot Christi* was a letter to the Editor of *The New Statesman* for 17 June 1916.

The Infidel Half Century is the title of Shaw's long Preface to *Back to Methuselah,* first printed in 1921, reprinted in the Standard Edition in 1931. The selection as here presented is a condensation. The excerpt from the play is from pp. 252–254.

**A Catechism on My Creed* was printed in the *St. Martin-in-the-Fields Review* for May 1922 under the heading 'Bernard Shaw on Religion'.

**The Infancy of God* and

**A Note on the Prayerbook* are both from typescript edited in Shaw's hand and marked by him 'Hitherto Unpublished'. They appear to have been composed about the same time as the following:

**On Ritual, Religion, and the Intolerableness of Tolerance* is also from edited typescript, but an extra copy bears the alternative title, 'The Church Versus Religion', and both are dated 'Ayot St. Lawrence. 16/10/22'.

The Preface to *Saint Joan* was published with the play in 1924. It was paired with *The Apple Cart* in the Standard Edition, 1932. The selection is from pp. 11–18.

**Personal Immortality* was Shaw's contribution to a newspaper discussion of 'Where Are the Dead?' It was in the *Daily News* of 6 June 1928.

The New Stanza for the National Anthem was probably comp-posed after Shaw's relationship with Sir Edward Elgar had developed an easy cordiality. That would have been after the first of the Malvern Festivals in 1929. The stanza was quoted by Blanche Patch, *Thirty Years with Bernard Shaw* (Gollancz, 1954) pp. 229–30; and in Hesketh Pearson's *GBS*, *Postscript* (Collins, 1951), p. 77. Archibald Henderson in his *George Bernard Shaw: Man of the Century* (New York, 1956) also quotes it on p. 876, but he gives the second line as 'All of our safety lies . . .'

The Adventures of the Black Girl in Her Search for God was separately issued in 1932. In the Standard Edition, 1934, it became *The Black Girl in Search of God and Lesser Tales*. Excerpts are from the latter edition pp. 33–37; 53–62; and 65–72.

The Letters of Shaw to Dame Laurentia McLachlan were in-cluded by the Benedictines of Stanbrook in their tribute to their Mother Abbess in the publication of *In A Great Tradi-tion* (New York, 1956). The letters selected here are from pp. 262–3, and 270–2.

The Preface to *On the Rocks* was first published in the Stan-dard Edition, 1934, in the volume *Too True to Be Good*, *Village Wooing*, and *On the Rocks*. The passage included here is from pp. 174–84.

'*In Good King Charles's Golden Days*' was separately pub-lished in 1939, with special illustrations by Felix Topolski. In the Standard Edition, 1946, it was included with *Geneva* and *Cymbeline Refinished*. Excerpts from the play are from pp. 177–9; 180–2.

The Preface to *Farfetched Fables* was published with *Buoyant Billions*, *Farfetched Fables*, and *Shakes versus Shav* in the Standard Edition, 1950. Passages quoted are from pp. 63; 65–7; 76–7; 80–1.

Sixteen Self Sketches was first printed in the Standard Edition, 1949. Quotation is from pp. 76–9.

Only one essay included by Shaw in his folder on 'Religion and Religions' has been completely omitted in this collection. It is *Where Darwin is Taboo: the Bible in America*, to which Shaw had added, 'the Dayton Trial'. It was written for *The New Leader* of 10 July 1925 and was a report on the John T.

Scopes 'evolution' trial. The editor found this piece largely topical except for some familiar sallies against ignorance and fundamentalism. On the old proof sheets which Shaw had re-edited for the proposed volume he had carefully altered Dayton, *Tennessee* to read Dayton, *Ohio*. The Tennessee reading was, of course, correct, though Dayton, Ohio, is easier to locate on the map. For the curious, the Shaw Society of London can again furnish a reprint, this time in its publication, *The Shavian* for September, 1960 (Vol. 2, No. 2) pp. 3–9 – with Dayton returned to the proper State.